CHINAMPAS

THEIR ROLE IN AZTEC EMPIRE – BUILDING & EXPANSION

AN ACADEMIC RESEARCH

INCLUDING A CHAPTER ON THE HISTORICAL BACKGROUND OF THE AZTECS AND THE VALLEY OF MEXICO.

ALFRED AGHAJANIAN

PREFACE

What comprises in this book is a humble effort in demonstrating the importance of the chinampa agricultural system in the Aztec empire. This effort is in form of a research project, undertaken to fulfill a part of the requirements for a master's degree in Latin American Studies at California State University, Los Angeles. My motive in publishing this research is the hope that it will be available to wider readers and will create further awareness and interest in the subject matter. I am confident that despite the shortcomings of this research project, students, scholars, as well as others from all walks of life who are interested in chinampas will benefit from this work. In addition to the content, the reader will especially benefit from the rich source of references. Theses sources are essential for understanding the chinampa farming system today, its role on Aztecs' life during the Aztec empire, as well as the history and various approaches of looking at the Aztecs rule in the Valley of Mexico.

THE ROLE OF CHINAMAPAS IN AZTEC EMPIR- BUILDING AND ITS EXPANSION

A Thesis
Presented to

The Faculty of Latin American Studies Program
California State University, Los Angeles

In Partial Fulfillment
of the Requirements for the Degree
Master of Arts

By
Alfred Aghajanian
December 2006

ACKNOWLEDGMENTS

The work on this thesis has been an inspiring, sometimes exciting, often challenging, but always interesting experience. It has been made possible by close associations with people who supported me.

I am very grateful to my supervisor, Marjorie Bray for her continuous guidance, advice, encouragement, support, positive assessments of the thesis drafts, her proofreading of numerous of thesis drafts, and helping me throughout my research project. It is definitely safe to say that without her dedicated involvement, this project would not have been possible.

I am in debt to Donald Bray, whom I consider my mentor and have had the fortune to know him for more than a decade. It was because of his effective oratory and teaching styles, as well as his pleasant personality in the political science courses, related to Latin America, that initially I got interested in Latin American Studies. As a member of my thesis committee his reassuring assessments during the course of submitting the drafts have particularly helped me in easing my stress associated with writing the thesis.

My sincere thanks to Eric Schantz, another member of my thesis committee, whose expertise in deciphering original pre-Columbian documents in a course taught me much in research projects. His inputs and his involvement in this thesis within his busy schedule are much appreciated.

I am very thankful to Phil Crossley, an expert in chinampa agricultural system. In our e-mail correspondence that started about two years ago, not only has he provided me directions with his wisdom on chinampa agriculture and with vital sources, but also he encouraged me with his advice as to how to use my time effectively during the approaching of the thesis deadline. I have greatly profited from hints, generously lavished in the course of our correspondence.

I would also like to express my gratitude to my long time professor and advisor at Portland State University, Jack Corbett. He has given me the chance to participate in many international trips involving comparative study of public administration. During the two visits to Mexico, knowing my interest in chinampa agriculture, he has supported me with his encouragement and many fruitful discussions about chinampas. His gesture of personally buying me the Teresa Rojas' *La Agricultura Chinampera* book in Mexico is sincerely appreciated.

Finally, I take this opportunity to express my profound gratitude to my beloved sisters whose engagements in their own serious studies have been an inspiration and a source of motivation in completing this thesis.

ABSTRACT

Chinampa Agricultural system, employed by Aztecs as the main form of agricultural system, has been shown as one of the most important variables in settlement of the nomadic Aztec tribes, expansion of the tribes, the Aztec state formation, and ultimately in Aztec empire-building and its expansion. Several relevant sources have been identified, through which inferences have been made using specific evidence, and inductive and deductive reasoning. The inferences made through these sources suggest the viability of the hypothesis of this research, that the chinampa agriculture was one of the most important elements in the Aztec empire building process.

TABLE OF CONTENTS

LIST OF FIQURES

x

CHAPTER 1

Introduction

The hypothesis of this thesis is that the role of the *chinampa* agriculture was one of the most important elements in the Aztec empire building process. The literature on Aztecs is simply overwhelming. It seems there are no aspects of Aztecs' life that have been left unexplored. There are numerous works on Aztecs' agriculture and on the chinampa system specifically. The works that I have encountered have not however specifically dealt with the direct role of chinampa agriculture in the Aztec empire building. Nevertheless, there is a vast body of literature on the chinampa system and the Aztecs that can be used to infer the importance and the vital role of the chinampa agricultural system in the Aztec empire building. This will be the main strategy of this research: that is, to use this abundant body of work logically to conclude, using mostly deductive reasoning and by tangible examples and cases, that the chinampa agricultural system had in fact a vital impact on the creation and expansion of the Aztec empire.

For example, from the Hagen's book entitled, *The Ancient Sun Kingdom of the Americas* (1961), this research will infer that one of the key factors that shapes any human society is its physical environment in which it is created and grows. In the beginning of thirteenth century when the Aztecs migrated to their new habitat, they found that all the arid lands were already taken by more powerful tribes than themselves. The Aztecs had no choice but to settle in the swamps and the marshlands of the area, a physical environment that was overlooked by the several other tribes, who thought that the swamps and marshland would not be a suitable environment in which to grow the crops that they needed for sustenance. However, it was the same "unsuitable" environment that gradually would come to make a great contribution in the strengthening and growth of the Aztec tribes, eventually leading them to become an empire. The Aztecs either by stroke of luck or by wisdom learned and adapted to the chinampa agricultural system in their swampy marshlands. Soon, not only could they sustain themselves, but they also could grow food surpluses, thanks to the system of Chinampa agriculture. These observations are an example of this research's use of various rich sources to infer the importance of the chinampa agriculture in the Aztecs' life and their empire-building.

Numerous works of authors such as Beltran's will be used to support the hypothesis of this research. Among these authors are M.D. Coe (1964), Teresa Rojas Rabiela (1993), William Sanders and Barbara J. Price (1968), Jeffrey R. Parsons and others (1982), Jeffrey R. Parsons and others (1985). Parsons' work entitled, *The Role of Chinampa Agriculture in the Food Supply of Aztec Tenochtitlan* (1976) comes close to giving the chinampa system of agriculture its due importance. However, his work, valuable as it is, is limited to the role of chinampas in providing food supply to Aztec Tenochtitlan, the center of the Aztec empire. Nevertheless Parsons' (1976) work is unparalleled in the context of lack of other research on the important role of chinampas in Aztec life. His work has been of great benefit to the project at hand here.

To appreciate the role of the Aztec economy, mainly the chinampa agricultural system, in Aztec expansion toward an empire, it is important to consider the Aztec religious ideology, especially in the context of warfare about which there are numerous sources, which will be used as references. Through theses sources it will be argued and subsequently shown that it was only with the increased production through chinampa agriculture that the Aztecs could not only sustain themselves but also accomplish this with less manpower, which freed a substantial segment of the society to become the warriors, priests, and merchants who made the difference between Aztecs and a number of other native tribes with less productive agricultural systems, thus making the Aztec empire possible. It is also important to acknowledge the credit due to the Aztecs' religious ideology in conducting warfare and expanding their territories. However, inferring from the above various sources this study's argument will be that without economic success, which was mainly based on the chinampa agricultural system, the Aztecs could not have had the luxury of acting, expanding, and reinforcing their religious ideology. Therefore, without sustenance from the chinampa agricultural system the Aztecs would probably have remained an obscure nomadic tribe as they had been before settling in the small islands in Lake Texcoco, surrounded by the marshlands and swamps that gave them the opportunity to adopt the practice of the ancient system of chinampa agriculture.

The bulk of the above mentioned sources on the Aztecs deal with the role of warfare, tributes, and commerce as the main factors of Aztec empire building. While acknowledging the importance of these three factors in Aztec empire building and expansion, this research will aim at digging, so to speak, deeper and conclude that behind each of these factors the chinampa agricultural system had a major role to play. For instance in the case of Aztecs' tributes this research will endeavor to show that the tributes themselves were as a result of chinampa agricultural productivity, which was an important factor in warfare and acquiring tributary subjects. Further more, the tributes themselves, in most cases, consisted of agricultural products through the chinampa system that sustained the Aztec empire. For example the Xochimilco region had suitable shallow lake sites with fresh water that made the region famous for its chinampa agricultural productivity. Once the Aztecs conquered the Xochimilco region, most likely because of the region's chinampa agricultural productivity, they imposed tributes that consisted of mostly agricultural and related products from chinampa fields of Xochimilco, which were essential in providing the large population of the Aztec urban centers, such as Tenochtitlan, their basic sustenance needed. Therefore, we should consider chinampa agricultural system as a major factor in sustaining and providing the Aztecs the opportunity to create their infrastructures and expand their rule in the Valley of Mexico and beyond.

The next chapter of this project deals with the general introduction of the chinampa agriculture system, so the readers who are not familiar with the chinampas will have the opportunity to familiarize themselves with this ancient, self sustaining, and productive system of agriculture. Chapter three will deal with the historical background of Aztecs and the Valley of Mexico in general. This information is vital in understanding the Aztecs, since the formation of the Aztec empire was ultimately a product of gradual evolutionary interactions between various political and social entities of the region.

Chapter four will discuss the role of chinampas in Aztec state formation. The chapter will deliberate on some theoretical underpinnings of state formation and look at the Aztecs' case through those theoretical frameworks, at the same time bringing to light the importance of the chinampa agricultural system in Aztec state formation. The chapter will include the pre-Aztec era and conclude with the formation of the Aztec empire. The expansion of the Aztec empire and the role of chinampa agricultural system through new centralized efforts in expanding the chinampa agriculture during the expansion period of Aztec empire will be the topic of chapter five.

In short, this research will use a large volume of sources written on various elements of Aztec empire and, inferring from those, will come to the conclusion that the chinampa agricultural system, which the Aztecs used, had a direct and important role in their empire building. Because of the huge volume of the resources on Aztecs, this research will inevitably be incomplete. The hope of this research is to create an awareness and interest in the specific role of the chinampa agricultural system in the Aztec empire-building and stimulate continued research on this matter.

CHAPTER 2

Chinampa Agriculture

Approaching the Basin of Mexico and the City of Tenochtitlan in 1519, Hernando Cortes and his men were amazed. They saw a sight that was difficult to believe. An astounding white city, anchored to the shores by three long causeways, floated on a glittering lake. Seville was the last city they had seen before sailing by ship to the "New World"; Seville was the largest city in Spain with more than sixty thousand inhabitants. This lake-borne city was almost four times as large, with thousands more people massed in the "suburbs" anchoring the mainland. The city, unlike the cramped muddle of houses, streets, and byways that made up medieval Spanish towns, had been planned. Unlike Seville there was no contamination of smoke or dirt. The structures were brilliant, and even the humblest dwellings, some of them with roof-gardens, were adorned and covered with colored stucco. Bernal Diaz, a Spanish foot soldier remembered the impact of the "enchanted vision" of this magical city. Bernal Diaz further recounts that:

> Next morning, we came to a broad causeway and continued our march towards Iztapalapa. And when we saw all those cities and villages built in the water, and other great towns on dry land, and that straight and level causeway leading to Mexico, we were astounded. These great towns and cues (temple-pyramids) and buildings rising from the water, all made of stone, seemed like an enchanted vision from the tale of Amadis. Indeed, some of our soldiers asked whether it was not all a dream. It is not surprising therefore that I should write in this vein. It was all so wonderful that I do not know how to describe this first glimpse of things never heard of, seen or dreamed of before (Diaz del Castillo, 1963 p. 216).

Cortes and his men also found the practice of a unique agricultural system. This method of farming, which still persists in limited intensity today, consists of land development through the construction of what is called *chinampas* in marshy areas and shallow lakes.

The chinampa system is a network of raised fields (*camellones*) on man-made low islands in the lakes and marshes. Chinampa is a derivative word from two Nauhatl language words (the language spok̫   cs) of *chinamitl*, meaning "reed bask   *pan*, meaning "upon", which ap   scribes the method of building the c˙   method consists of piling lake bed aquatic plants and dry-land crop silted muck and manures in precise reed fences secured in the bottom of marshlands. Once the ground was per height, fast growing willow trees re planted on the edges, which erosion of the raised ground. These so provided shade and firewood, and e crop-damaging pests. Chinampa known as *"chinampanecas,"* or more *chinamperos"* (Werner, 1992). g to Coe (1964), while the farmers or dig out canals in the lake-bed, they e mud, which they scoop out, atop reeds. These assembled masses, which led by water on at least three sides, are and serve as the garden plots in which the chinamperos grow their crops. In the masses homes were also constructed on the top of these chinampas. These chinampas were between fifteen and thirty feet wide and 300 feet long and were a few feet above the water level.

Chinampas are sometimes mistakenly called "floating gardens". When Hernan Cortes and his men entered in the Valley of Mexico in 1519, they passed through the chinampa-lined causeway at Chuitlahuac on their way to Tenochtitlan. When planning to besiege the Tenochtitlan two years later, he took control of these chinampas. In a letter to Charles V, Cortes described Chuitlahuac "the best looking small city we have seen," and noted that Mixquic (another chinampa settlement in the chinampa zone) was "a small town, completely set upon water." (Werner, 1992 p.17). The first Spaniards to document the chinampas in detail were responsible for creating the "floating garden" myth, which still remains to this day. The author of the "Historia Natural y Moral de las Indias", José de Acosta, described that "chinampas were towed from place to place like barges." Even the "clear-sighted" geologist and naturalist Alexander von Humbolt, after seeing buoyant mats of "water hyacinch"[1], accepted the idea of the floating chinampa story, which the Spaniards themselves had introduced (Werner, 1992 p.17).

---

[1] In Greek mythology, Hyacinth (in Greek, Ύάκινθος — Hyakinthos) was a divine hero.

Steps in Constructing Chinampas

Prutzman (1988) outlined seven steps in chinampa construction. First, chinamperos use a long pole to find an adequate base for a chinampa and when possible use the remains of an old chinampa (called *cimiento*), as the foundation. Second, robust reeds are "stuck" in the bottom to mark the base dimensions. Next, farmers dig mud from around the base and pile it on the top of the reeds and cimiento. Fourth, strips of water vegetation are cut and towed to the new chinampa. These dense vegetative strips are principally water lily and tule (Outerbridge, 1987). Fifth, a compost deposit is created by layering the strips of vegetation on top of each other until there is a thick covering of vegetation. Sixth, mud from the bottom of the lake is mixed with soil from an old chinampa and placed on top, reaching a height of about one foot above the water level. Hence an absorptive base rich in organic matter is created through which water easily flowed. Lastly, the sides are fenced with woven reeds, and then willow trees (*Salix bomplandiana*), are planted around the edges (See figure 2.1) (Prutzman, 1988).

Wilken (1985) presents an alternative view of chinampa construction. Wilken suggests that aquatic plants have no structural role in chinampas; rather, he asserts that plots are constructed by "simply extending drainage canals out into swamps or shallow lakes or back into low-lying shores" and then placing the excavated material onto spaces between the canals. While the dredged mud inevitably will contain aquatic plants, Wilken believes that these plants are not important structural components of chinampa building.

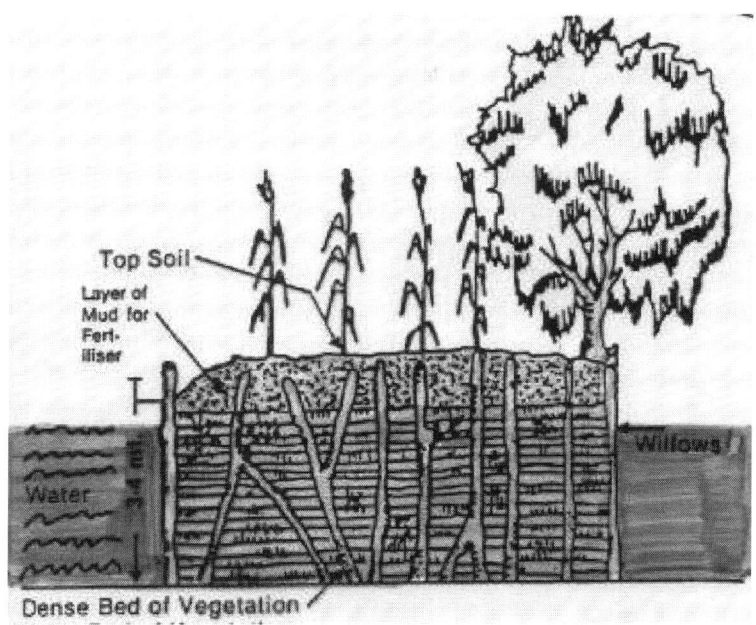

Figure 2.1 Elements in constructing chinampas
Retrieved August 20, 2006, from:
http://www.geog.psu.edu/courses/geog103/aglect1.h
tm

Regardless of the method of chinampa construction, it is obvious that chinampas are highly adequate at absorbing moisture. In these man-made islets, the porosity of the soil allows seepages from the surrounding canals to keep the soil continuously moist at the root level providing continuous irrigation. This constant irrigation by seepage allows year-round cultivation in the chinampa system, even through the dry season of the year (Armillas, 1971). In the rare cases that conditions became too dry for adequate penetration of moisture, the chinamperos can resort to hand-watering their plants.

The canals are populated with abundant wildlife, fish, crustaceans, waterfowl, and salamanders to name a few, which provided the natives an important part of their diet. They also serve as corridors for the farmers' flat-bottomed canoes (Coe, 1964). To insure that their crops have a fertile environment in which to grow, the chinamperos also excavate mud from the lake bottom with a *zoquimaitl* (canvas bag attached to the end of a long pole), transport it to the chinampa with their canoes, and spread it on the chinampa surface. (See figure 2.2) This is often done before each planting. Farmers often have a favorite spot for obtaining nutrient-rich mud (Prutzman, 1988). Chinamperos also periodically scrape off the surface soil of their chinampas. This is either to remove soil that is salty or to lower chinampa height for the crop roots to have adequate access to moisture (Parsons et al, 1985).

Chinamperos use their minimal land very efficiently. With the exception of maize, chinamperos do not sow seeds directly into the chinampas; rather they use the technique of the

Figure 2.2 The chinamperos excavating mud from the lake bottom with zoquimaitls Retrieved August 20, 2006, from:
http://geography.berkeley.edu/programcourses/cour sepagesfa2004/geog148/Term%20Papers/Sanaz%20 Memasadeghi/whatis.htm

seed nursery or *almacigo*. According to Warner (1992), this was the Aztec's greatest innovation in the chinampa agricultural system. It allowed chinamperos to take care of the crops at their most delicate stage. Coe (1964) furnishes a clear description of the almacigo technique.

> The nursery... is made by spreading a thick layer of mud over a bed of waterweeds. After several days, when the mud is hard enough, it is cut into little rectangular blocks called *chapines*. [See figure 2.3] The *chinampero* makes a hole in each *chapine* with a finger, a stick or a small ball of rag, drops in the seed and covers it with manure, which now comes from cattle but in Aztec days came from humans... Finally each seedling is transplanted in its own *chapin* to a place on the chinampa, which has been cultivated and leveled with a spade or hoe (the Aztecs employed a digging stick called a *coa*) and then covered with canal mud (Coe, 1964 p. 94).

Chinampas were not an Aztec invention. "Earlier evidence is found in the nearby ancient city of Teotihuacan and among the lowland Maya, as well as in Suriname's swamps and Peru's Lake

Titicaca… [However] it was under Aztec rule that they were most extensively built and intensively cultivated." (Werner, 1992 p.2).

Figure 2.3 Chapines in almacigo technique
Retrieved August 20, 2006, from:
http://geography.berkeley.edu/programcourses/cour
sepagesfa2004/geog148/Term%20Papers/Sanaz%2M
emasadeghi/whatis.htm

Early References to Chinampas

The chinampa system was described by number of Spanish colonial writers from the 16th century onward. In freshwater lagoons wrote one of them, the Indians "without much trouble plant and harvest their maize and greens, for all over are ridges called chinampas; these are strips built above water and surrounded by ditches, which obviates watering" (Torquemada, 1723 as cited in Armillas, 1971 p. 653).

The pattern and procedures for the laying of chinampas and the essentials of chinampa farming system were outlined in the following excerpts from 16th century documents:

> They make garden plots...carrying in canoes sod cut in the mainland, to heap it up in shallow waters, thus forming ridges from 3 to 4 varas wide [about 2.52 to 3.36 meters] and raised half a vara above the water; a farm has many of these ridges, and the farmers circulate in their canoes between them (Machuca, 1599 as cited in Armillas, 1971 p. 653).

To tend the crops,

> ...these plots are...built upon the water by heaping sod from land and mud from the lagoon, forming very narrow strips...separated by canals

and, as these gardens are raised less than a vara above the water, even without rainfall they bear vigorous maize, sustained by the moisture provided by the lagoon... and...they set maize seedbeds on the chinampas and they transplant the seedlings, which is a thing peculiar to that country (Ponce, 1723 as cited in Armillas, 1971 p. 653).

According to yet another witness these moveable nurseries were:

...20 to 30 feet long and is broad as the farmers deems convenient, laid on rush, cattail, and sward; on these they set seedbeds for vegetables which are to be transplanted later, and they tow them with ropes from one place to another within the lagoon (Ojea, 1897 as cited in Armillas, 1971 p. 653).

The legend of so called floating gardens may have arisen with errors of observation made by some of these witnesses who apparently mistook the movable nurseries for the farm plots. As the above observations make clear, the layout of the chinampas was constructed mainly to capture moisture. Standing waters of the lake or marshes were critical for operation of the chinampa system.

Chinampas Today and the Efforts to Preserve Them

The chinampa agricultural system survived the conquest and the subsequent Spanish and Mexican detrimental policies towards it, although much limited as to the scope and quality. The Spaniards being horsemen did not care much for the "hydrological talents" of farmers and demolished most of the chinampa system, "the Aztec's finest water works", in one way or another throughout the centuries. "In their most brazen act, they [the Spaniards] stole stores [sic] from Nezalmalcoytl's great dike in order to erect their colonial city upon Tenochtitlan's ruins." The result was that disastrous flooding occurred, and it continued to plague the city until well into the 20th century. Rather than controlling the water as Aztecs had done, the Spaniards' way of dealing with these floods was to attempt to eliminate them altogether through a series of ambitious drainage designs that ultimately remained ineffective. They reasoned that chinampas would be emptied and that the lake bottoms would make rich farmland. However, they did not know that the lakes were mostly saline. The storms of harmful ground salts "wind-whipped like dust off drying beds" would come to rival flooding as Mexico City's worst natural affliction (Werner, 1992 p. 11).

Lakes Xochimilco and Chalco, even though fed by underground springs, began slowly to shrink, resulting in the disappearance of many of the chinampas over the next centuries. The Amecameca, Tenango, and Tlalmanalco rivers, which were supplying Lake Chalco's fresh water, were diverted by the Spaniards; as a result by the 1900s the lake was dried, except in times of heavy rain. Even more alarming for the already disappearing chinampas was the decision by President Porfirio Díaz to tap into Xochimilco's largest springs. The plan began with Nativitas[2] and by 1930 included La Noria, Acalpixca, and Tlaxiatemalco. The purpose of the plan was to supply fast growing Mexico City with drinking water. As a result, Lake Xochimilco began to shrink even further, and by 1950 the chinampas had almost totally disappeared.

The survival of these limited chinampas (See figure 2.4) was due in most part to the Xochimilcans' and Chalcans' cultural boldness. When starting in the 1950's the chinamperos organized and staged protests, the officials finally acted. However, their solution to the problem was not adequate. They merely redirected semi-treated sewage water in the

---

[2] The name Nativitas refers to lakes that formerly existed in the Valley of Mexico, on which the inhabitants cultivated chinampas.

chinampa areas of Xochimilco, through the Canal Nacional, which amassed untreated industrial and household wastes. The declining water quality caused chinampa productivity to decrease dramatically. By 1988, only half of the chinampas' remaining 2,300 hectares were intensely farmed, and more than twenty useful plant species had disappeared in just about two decades (Werner, 1992 p. 13).

The current situation is of grave concern to José Genovevo Pérez. José is a chinampero in Xochimilco's Pueblo de San Luis Tlaxialtemalco and one of the leaders of a grassroots chinampa preservation campaign. José maintains that chinamperos still do not get enough water to keep the canals full, and the little they do get is too dirty. José is happy that UNESCO declared Xochimilco a World Heritage Site in 1988. Jose is right; as a result of the UNESCO's act there is a renewed attention on the chinamperos' dilemma. As a result in 1989 the Mexican government launched the Ecological Rescue Plan. But according to José

> ...The chinampas are endangered, and we want everyone to know we've got to do more to save them... Even our schoolbooks forget there are still chinamperos alive today. We're not history yet (Werner, 1992 p.13).

Werner (1992, p. 16) credits Arturo Gómez-Pompa, a

Figure 2.4 Existing chinampa plots at Xochimilco, Federal District, Mexico. (With permission: Phil Crossley,
http://www.western.edu/faculty/pcrossley)

According to professor Crossley, this particular photo is an interesting one, in that it shows a chinampa that is probably more like the older, traditional ones, than just about any other in Xochimilco today since the canal is fairly narrow and that the farmer is growing corn. It also shows well the fact that the trees are not 'anchoring the field to the bottom of the lake' as so many have claimed. For more information refer to the website above and Crossley (2004).

conservation-minded botanist as being most responsible for alerting the outside world to the chinampa as an ecologically-sound farming model. Gómez-Pompa has been involved in chinampa advocacy and research for more than two decades. His work with the National Research Institute of Biotic Resources, or INIREB[3], based in Veracruz, has resulted in tangible progress in preservation of the chinampa agricultural system.

> As Gomez-Pompa saw it the challenges was to modify and then transfer the chinampa system, long adapted to the climate and soil of Mexico's temperate highlands, to marginal sites in his country's tropical lowlands in order to increase food production while preserving the environment. This idea's feasibility was underscored by archeological evidence from Belize's Pulltrouser Swamp and the Yucatan's Candelaria Basin showing that the Mayans also had once farmed raised fields (camellones) (Werner, 1992 p. 14).

---

[3] National Research Institute of Biotic Resources (In Spanish: Instituto Nacional de Investigación sobre Recursos Bióticos [INIREB]) was founded in 1975 by Arturo Gómez-Pompa who pioneered research in agroecology, analyzing the agricultural techniques used by people inhabiting the rain forests in his native country of Mexico.

Subsequently chinamperos assisted in construction of test plots in coastal swamps and lagoons in Veracruz and Tabasco. Some plots were unsuccessful and were abandoned; others however steadily took hold and elicited broad national and international interest. The most successful of these chinampa plots belong to Chontal Indians, located near the capital of Tabasco. However, the chinampas in Chontal plots apply a modified chinampa technology of the Mayan forest garden system known as *"Pet kot"*, a smaller mixed-use area of fruit trees and food crops. In Chontal chinampa plots, the aquatic plants are composted as fertilizer; however other standard chinampa practices, such as preparing and maintaining soil, are not followed. Hence,

> Even though Gomez-Pompa sees that chinampa building and farming techniques cannot be transferred wholesale from one place to another, he feels they do provide a model for reclaiming and using marginal areas in otherwise land scarce regions (Werner, 1992 p. 15).

While the chinampa agricultural system might be a viable ecological and economic practice elsewhere, questions still remain about the future of the original plots of chinampas in Xochimilco. Should we consider these chinampas as just a monument to Mexico's past, or are they agriculturally still viable in this day and age? Considering Mexico's huge amount of food needs, some experts consider them as archaic and bygone as the tiny patches of corn still planted in the city. On the other hand one estimate suggests that because of the chinampas high yield and year-round productivity, they could potentially satisfy one quarter of Mexico City's need for fresh vegetables (Werner, 1992 p. 16). It is estimated that only ten to twenty percent of the chinampa lands that Aztecs cultivated in the early sixteenth century remain in use today and much of these remaining chinampas are endangered by inadequate water supply and the encroachment of pollution from Mexico City (Feinman, 1997 p. 328).

Stemming from an international meeting of natural scientists, social scientists, and chinamperos held in April 1990, a book came out called, *Presente, Pasado, y Futuro de las Chinampas*, edited by well-known contemporary chinampa expert, Teresa Rojas Rabiela.[4] This collection centered broadly on a four-point plan, which involves legislation, economic stimulation, investigation, and the recognition of social and cultural concerns. The plan is designed to

---

[4] Teresa Rojas Rabiela is an expert on chinampas. She is the editor of *La Agricultura Chinampera: Compiliacion historica*. Universidad Autonoma Chapingo, 1993, which is an important volume among her several works on chinampa agricultural system.

protect the chinampas and the people who still depend on them (Feinman, 1997 pp. 328-329).

Chinampas today, despite their limitations, are testaments to the ingenuity and skills of pre-Columbian agricultural science. Fortunately in recent years with the dedicated work of chinampa experts such as Arturo Gómez-Pompa and Teresa Rojas Rabiela we are beginning to realize the value of this ancient farming system. New initiatives have been adopted, not only in preserving what little of chinampas that are left, but also expanding them in terms of developing test plots around the country, where the local environment is likely to benefit from the chinampa agricultural system.

Although there have been some positive steps in preservation of the existing chinampas, the overall picture of long-term survival of these chinampas is not guaranteed or even promising. Whenever a chinampa parcel is abandoned, with it the entailed knowledge of chinampa science is irrevocably erased. Hence if we anguish over the loss of any plant and animal species when the rainforest is cut, we must also anguish over the loss of this ancient knowledge of planting as the chinampas are relegated to oblivion.

CHAPTER 3

Historical Background of Aztecs and the Valley of Mexico

The Aztec empire that the Spaniards encountered in the 16th century was the most recent and shortest of an estimated 3,000 years of settlement in Mesoamerica.[5] (See also figure 3.1) To understand Aztec history one must consider the antecedent events that influenced the Aztec supremacy in the region. It is illogical to separate the Aztec history from that of the region's general history, since Aztecs had inherited most of their cultural practices from their Mesoamerican

---

[5] The term Mesoamérica is used to refer to a geographical region that extends roughly from the Tropic of Cancer in central Mexico down through Guatemala, Belize, Honduras, El Salvador, and Nicaragua to northwestern Costa Rica, and which is characterized by the particular cultural homogeneity that the indigenous cultures in this region exhibit. As such it is a cultural area, defined by the cultural similarities that have spread between the different cultures of the area through millennia of interaction.

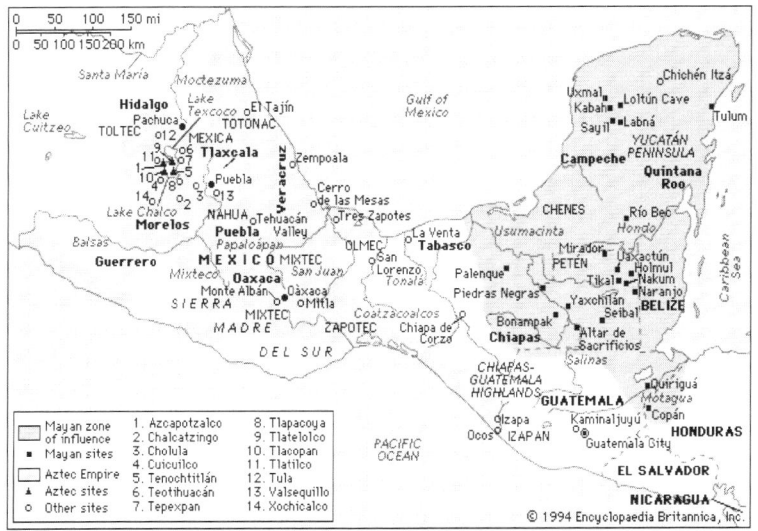

Figure 3.1   The region of Mesoamerica, with boundaries and regions of major civilizations and city states. Retrieved August 20, 2006, from: http://www.crystalinks.com/olmec.html

predecessors. Hence for a complete picture of the Aztec history we must trace the cultural patterns of their life well before the history of Aztec "statehood", from their tribal migration, to the Toltec (900-1170 C.E.), and even further back to the great civilization of Teotihuacan (200 B.C.E. - 750 C.E.), which had its roots in earlier complex societies that first developed in Mesoamerica around 1500

B.C.E.[6] For the purpose of this project however, I will start by focusing on Toltecs, the people with whom the Aztecs had a particular affinity (Berdan, 2005; Townsend, 1992).

The Toltec Precedent

The Toltec capital of Tula dwindled around 1,170 C.E.; the event was an antecedent for displacement and migration of people in the highlands. Some found themselves in the region located in the southern Valley of Mexico; others migrated to northern ranges from where they began their long and gradual path to arrive at the central plateau. Although our understanding of the Toltecs is limited, nevertheless from their archeological remains we can infer that Toltec society conclusively had extensive political and cultural influence in the region (Healan, 1989). The Toltec empire collapsed about 250 years before the prominence of Aztec state; however Tula, the capital of the Toltecs, was still considered as a "center of power and civilization." And its heritage commanded considerable respect among the urban populations. To be a Toltec "was synonymous with being 'civilized'." (Townsend, 1992 p. 44).

---

[6] Mesoamerican history is roughly divided into four periods: Archaic (7,000 B.C.E - 2,000 B.C.E.), Pre-classic or formative (2,000 B.C.E. - 250 C.E.), Classic (250 C.E. – 900 C.E.), and Post-classic (900 C.E. – 1521 C.E.).

In the later wave of migration in the 13th century, there were several migrant groups who began to arrive to the Valley or basin of Mexico (Aztecs called the valley Anahuac) (See figure 3.2). The Valley of Mexico contains:

> …some 700 cubic km. in area. The region extends from the eastern edge of Lake Texcoco east to the foothills of the Sierra Madre Oriental. Its southern edge is defined by a line of high hills and its northern edge by spur of the Sierra Madre; to the north of this spur is the Valley of Teotihuacán." (Michels, 1973 p. 117).

Four of these migrant groups would later play a crucial role in the creation of the Aztec state and ultimately the rise of Aztec empire. "The traditional histories of these groups reflect the official version prepared long after the actual migrations." (Townsend, 1992 p. 51). These reports were again chronicled in the early Spanish colonial histories of native peoples. Most of these accounts of the migrations were written by the descendants of the Indian nobility. The "official" interpretations of the migration stories reflect how the Aztecs and their neighboring tribes manipulated the historical events by interweaving legends with actual happenings, at times proclaiming supposedly extraordinary events that in reality were directly borrowed from much earlier civilizations. We can be fairly confident that these efforts show the aspiration of the new migrants for an acceptable, that is noble, ancestry to elevate themselves and justify their superior status among other tribes and legitimize their effort to rule over the others (Aguilar, 2006; Berdan, 2005; Townsend, 1992).

The first major migrants were *Chichimecs*. The term Chichimec is also widely used to refer to all the immigrant groups. It is said that Chichimecs were led by a chieftain called Xolotl, whom one may view as a semi-legendary personification of various tribal leaders who are glorified in various ways in different histories. *Tepanecs* were a second group that probably originated in the valley of Tuluca and the Matlazinca and Mazahua ethnic stock of that region. The Tepanecs intermarried with the native people of the Valley of Mexico and in time settled at Atzcapotzalco, located on the western side of the Mexican basin. The *Acolhua* were the third major migrant group. They moved into the eastern side of the Mexican basin, which was then an uninhabited territory.

Thus, by the time the fourth major group reached the valley in the mid 13th century, very little land remained unoccupied in the basin. This fourth and last major group was a mixture of various other groups, intermarried together. They

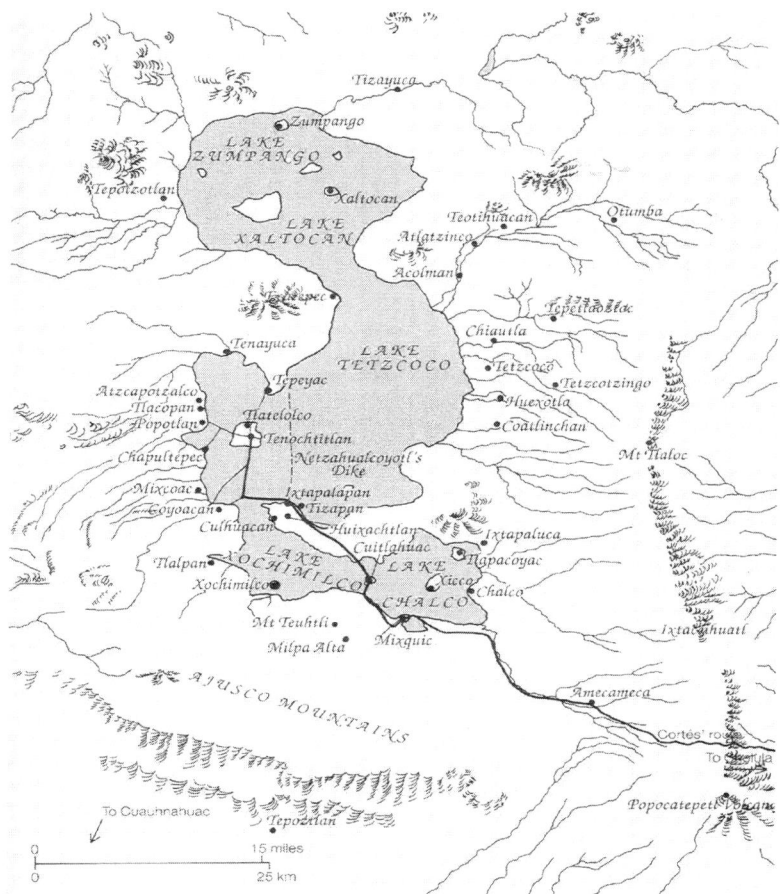

Figure 3.2 The valley of Mexico [in the era of Aztec empire]. The island city of Tenochtitlan-Tlatelolco was linked to the mainland by causeways, and protected from the brackish water of Lake Tetzcoco by Netzahulcoyotl's dike. Lake Chalco and Xochimilco to the south were fed by great springs and were the site of major chinampa plantations. (Figure and caption source: Townsend, 1992 p. 27)

eventually settled on the island that later became Tenochtitlan and declared themselves the *Mexica*. The interactions of these groups of newcomers with the "original" settlers resulted in major and dynamic changes in the region in the 15th century (Townsend, 1992 p. 51).

The events regarding the migration of Chichimecs and Acolhua is attested in the 16th century colonial pictorial manuscripts, such as the Codex Xolotle, Mapa Quinatzin, and Codex Aubin, and also in the written history of the 17th century historian, Fernando de Alva Ixtlilxochtl. Both the codices and the written texts are derived from earlier pictorial manuscripts as well as oral histories. These sources describe a rather plain melodramatic version of the events, which in reality were an entangled course of adjustment of the new immigrants to the more urbanized civilization of the "original" people of the valley (Townsend, 1992 p. 51).

The Mexica

The early history of the Mexica tribe is the most well known and written about compared to all other migrant groups. According to Townsend (1992, p. 55), "The legends of their [Mexica] origins, travels, and adventures, and their various settlements and battles before founding Tenochtitlan are recorded in the school books of Mexico today." As was above alluded to, the orthodox story of the Mexicas' migration was composed from various earlier written and pictorial sources. In these descriptions the "facts" are mostly expressed in metaphoric terms, at times describing magical or extraordinary events that cannot be substantiated with confidence. Hence, many questions still remain as to the Mexica tribe's original place, the time of their departure, the advancing route of their journey, and the importance of certain events and places that are mentioned in the textual sources. Many researchers, such as Gillespie (1989 p. xvii as cited in Townsend, 1992), regard the Mexica migration as a:

> …composite of stories assembled by a small tribe after arriving and intermarrying in the Valley of Mexico, since many motifs in these stories have a long earlier history among the original urban tribes in the Valley of Mexico (Townsend, 1992 p. 54).

Legend or fact, it is immensely important to recognize that the Aztecs, especially after establishing Tenochtitlan, thought of these stories as historical fact. These legendary stories took root early on in Mexica collective imagination, inspiring their ambitions, standards, and eventually affecting their thought processes leading to actions that proved to be pivotal in gradually establishing the Aztec empire.

Aztlan, the Origin of Mexica

The legend has it that during the early 12th century a tribe left from its ancestral homeland. The homeland is described to be an island within a lagoon, located somewhere unspecific to the north. The name of the place was *Aztlan,* meaning the place of cranes. From this name the archaic name *Aztec* was taken. It was only later during their migration that the people of Aztlan assumed the name *Mexica.* The original term, Aztec, reemerged again in scholastic studies of the 18th and 19th centuries, and it is now the accepted and generic name for the various peoples of the Valley of Mexico at the time of the Spanish Conquest (Townsend, 1992 p. 55).

Fray Diego Durán, in his recordings of oral history of the Mexica tribe, writes that the tribe had originally emerged from caves or springs in the time of genesis (Duran, 1967 pp. 217-218). According to Townsend (1992, p. 55), this version of the emergence of the Mexica is a localized version of an essentially universal motif in Mesoamerican mythology, which relates to the birth of people from the female earth, "the primordial mother of things". The legend chronicles Aztlan as an island that was set amidst reeds in the middle of a lagoon.

The geographical location of this supposed place called Aztlan has been widely debated among modern scholars, who believe in the existence of Aztlan. Many other archeologists and scholars still debate about whether the island called Aztlan ever existed. Some of these latter scholars argue that the story is a legend and denotes a mythological place that symbolizes Aztec historical creation. Those scholars who have attempted to locate the geographical location of Aztlan have not been successful in their attempt. Some speculate that the "south western area of the United States, the northwest part of Mexico, or the western area of Mexico are the possible location from which the Mexica originally departed" (Aguilar, 2006 p. 29).

The migration legend chronicles a route of travel to two major sites, *Culhuacan* (Curved Mountain) and *Chicomoztoc* (Seven Caves). The locations of these sites are unclear. There is, however, agreement among some scholars that the two sites lie somewhere between 60 and 180 miles to the northwest of the Valley of Mexico.[7] According to Kirchhoff (1961) the seven caves, Chicomoztoc, were in reality a feature of the curved mountain Culhuacan. Townsend (1992) writes that the manuscript "Historia Tolteca-Chichimeca" describes that formerly migratory tribes had settled in Chicomoztoc, before continuing on to settle in Puebla-Tlaxcala. The manuscript describes Culhuacan-Chicomoztoc as a "mountain with womb-like caves, representing the ancient notion of the mountain as a procreative entity." (Townsend

---

[7] The mountain Culhuacan is not to be confused with the town Culhuacan in the Valley of Mexico.

1992, p.57) (See Figure 3.3). Townsend continues that:

> The manuscript portrays a Chichimec priest enacting a creation myth, symbolically bringing forth the tribes from the earth as a sign of their passage from hunting and gathering in the search for a new place of agriculture (Townsend 1992, p.57).

Ultimately, when the Mexica arrived in the Valley of Mexico, they made their way to the area adjacent to the western lake side. They stopped temporarily at Tenayuca and continued on by Atzcapotzalco to arrive at Chapultepec; they populated the area near the springs at the base of the hill in Chapultepec in 1300 C.E. The following 25 to 45 years was a critical period for the Mexica. Unlike the Chichimec and Acolhua who had settled on tracts of uninhabited land, and unlike the Tepanecs who had migrated previously and had intermarried and integrated in the old town of Atzcapotzalco, the Mexica encountered unfriendly and contemptuous treatment. The first threat came from Copil, the leader of one of the towns, Malinalco, who began to conspire with the older towns to throw out the Mexica. As a result, the Mexica were chased out from Chapultepec.

Figure 3.3 The seven caves, Chicomoztoc
(Historia Tolteca-Chichimeca, p.11)
Retrieved   August 20, 2006, from:
http://www.geocities.com/Athens/Atrium/9449/s
17jcbr.htm

From this point on, according to Townsend (1992, p.60), the migration myth entered the sphere of confirmed history. Returning to Chapultepec once again, the Mexica soon encountered another threat. The new threat was from a coalition led by the Tepanecs of Atzcapotzalco and neighboring Culhuacan. The coalition aimed at mainly regaining control of the plentiful springs at Chapultepec. The Mexica were once again defeated in the area of modern Chapultepec Park in Mexico City. They dispersed around the countryside and nearby marshes of the lagoon.

Eventually, though, the Mexica made their way to Culhuacan and begged protection from its rulers. The Culhuacan elders granted the Mexica some land at Tizaapan, near today's University City. During their stay there the Mexica tribe displayed courage and endurance. Using their experiences as hunter and gatherers, they adapted to this harsh environment. They built small agricultural plots among the cliffs and boulders. Gradually they seemed to be more accepted by the Culhuacan, and courtship and intermarriages became common.

At this point the Mexica started regarding themselves as "Culhua-Mexica", and because of their newly established bonds of kinship, they began to see themselves as a part of Toltec civilization, for Culhuacan was a town where Toltec refugees had found refuge after the fall of Tula. An event had the potential to further strengthen the position of

Mexica within Culhuacan. In a small-scale war the Mexica participated as allies with Culhuacan against neighboring Xochimilco, and they were instrumental in winning the war. Initially the Culhua rulers were impressed with the Mexica military abilities. However they soon became dismayed by the Mexica, when as evidence of their attainment, the Mexica presented the Culhua rulers with collection of ears from Xochimilco warriors captured or killed in the battle. The audacity of the Mexica did not impress the Culhua nobles who viewed the Mexica as barbarous inferiors and began to feel uneasy regarding the Mexica's warlike nature. As a result, a consultation started among the Culhua nobles regarding the future of the Mexica as dwellers in their domain (Townsend, 1992 p. 61).

The Mexica realizing the growing tension and anticipating their violent departure, approached Achitometl, one of the Culhua nobles, and asked for his daughter as their "sovereign". Achitometl considered the offer as an honor and accepted it, sending his daughter to Tizaapan, where she was elegantly displayed and then sacrificed to the Huitzilopochtli.[8] The skin of the bride was peeled off, and a priest wore the skin in an ancient agricultural rite symbolizing the renewal of life. The unsuspecting Achitometl, who was invited to

---

[8] In Aztec mythology Huitzilopochtli, also spelled Uitzilopochtli, (the Nahuatl word for hummingbird), was a god of war and a sun god.

participate in the concluding festivities, unexpectedly recognized the skin of his daughter on the body of the priest. What ensued was that the outraged Achitometl joined with other Culhua nobles and threw the Mexica out of their domain. Once again the Mexica found themselves retreating into the reeds and repugnant swamps of Lake Tetzcoco, and from there across the water to an uninhibited island (Townsend, 1992 pp. 61).

The legend has it that when Mexica arrived in the reed beds, one of Huitzilopochtli's priests had a vision in which the ancestral deity appeared, informing him that a sacred place where the Mexica would have to settle was located somewhere near and was marked by a large nopal (prickly pear) cactus upon which an eagle would perch, devouring a serpent. Sure enough next morning they saw an eagle on the cactus, and they quickly erected a platform with a reed hut temple as the shrine of their tribal deity (see figure 3.4) (Aguilar, 2006 p.60; Townsend, 1992 p. 62).

This crude shrine was the precursor of the Great Pyramid of Tenochtitlan that would eventually be built. Thus, the Mexica claimed the island as their permanent home. They called it Tenochtitlan which refers to *teth* (rock), *nochtli* (cactus), and *tlan* (the location suffix). The founding of Tenochtitlan and later the neighboring settlement of *Tlatelolco* brought the Mexica's long migration to an end. The Mexica now had their permanent place that they could call their own. The place was surrounded by aggressive neighbors, but it also had positive aspects. Birds, fish, and many other animals were abundant. The

Figure 3.4   The vision of an eagle perched on a cactus devouring a serpent. Retrieved August 20, 2006, from:
http://www.artehistoria.com/historia/obras/9972.htm

lake shore was easily traveled by canoes, a very effective way to communicate and transport (Townsend, 1992 pp. 62-63). Efforts were also made to construct Chinampa system, which later played a major role in sustenance aside from hunting the wild animals.

Eventually Tenochtitlan grew in size and population. The 16th century historian, Fray Diego Duran describes the Mexica at this juncture as follows:

> They began to fill their city with people from neighboring towns and to take them in marriage. In this way they won over the people of Tetzcoco and others. They treated travelers and strangers well, they invited merchants to come to the markets of Mexico with their goods for such commerce always enriches a city (and this same Aztec nation today has this quality; for to towns where a man is well received and flattered and given to eat and drink he will go willingly, especially if he sees inviting faces, which is what most appeals to him) (Duran, 1964 p. 44).

I am not satisfied with Duran's explanation of the Aztec success in establishing and expanding their city state, even in that particular juncture of their history. The Mexica had to overcome overwhelming difficulties to ensure their survival. Perhaps their social organization and their political actions played a more vital role in Mexica success.

The Social Organization of Mexica

Almost all of the Native American societies were democratic. The land belonged to their communities and not to individuals. Most decisions were made by popular consent. Once individuals in these Native American groups began to sustain themselves through agriculture, they became members of a commune. This commune could be a clan or sib (kin, related by blood), as was the case with the Plains Indians, or an *ayllu* as among Incas, or it could be a *calpulli* (from *calli*, "house") as it was among the Aztecs. A member of the Mexica tribe was born into calpulli. A calpulli was a group household in an extended family. The land belonging to these households was held communally. For example a married man was lent a piece of land directly from the *calpulli*. No one owned the land that he worked on; he was only allowed to work and produce from the land; if he died, or the land was neglected, or he was thrown out of his *calpulli*, the land reverted back to communal ownership. According to Hagen (1961, p.69),

So exact were some of these, that records were kept on *amatl* paper of various land tracts along with a rebus drawing of the holder's name. According to their records there were seven original *calpulli,* once they settled on their island state, Tenochtitlan, these were enlarged into twenty."

Initially each of these calpulli owned or held lands by treaty on the mainland. The agricultural land was limited on the mainland. New calpulli members industriously created land by making chinampas. With this ingenious and hard labor of creating chinampas, a calpulli could extend its clan holdings and enlarge its production. In this way, gradually the calpullis were increasing in size and numbers. After the founding of Tenochtitlan, within the four-quarter plot of the city, each calpulli was assigned its own place, with its own temple and local cults.

As the Mexica leaders began to intermarry with the nobility of neighboring towns, the community, in terms of socioeconomic classes, became increasingly stratified. The *tlatoani* (speaker or "he who speaks") and *pipiltin* (nobles) controlled a vast amount of lands or income from the lands, owned directly or eventually captured in wars. Thus, they gradually acquired a basis of economic power that was independent from calpullis. In the early years of establishing Tenochtitlan the calpulli system made the private control of land unlikely. However in later years as the practice of war began to increase, private land ownership became a principal reward for the rising warrior class, as well as a major instrument in changing the economy (Townsend, 1992 p. 65).

The Birth of an Empire

After the founding of Tenochtitlan in 1325[9] to the time of the Spanish appearance in 1519, the Mexica aimed to assume a role for themselves in the physical as well as the sociopolitical environment of the Valley of Mexico. Their efforts can be seen as a dynamic course of adjustment to an atmosphere that was at times hospitable and at other times hostile. From 1325 t0 1428, the Mexica were subject to the dynamics of the valley that had been played from earlier times. The Mexica were at this period dominated by their stronger neighbors. At that stage the Mexica aspired essentially to adapt to existing patterns. From 1428 to 1519, however, they took a more proactive and imperial position, actively

---

[9] According to Hagen (1961, p. 60), "Tenochtitlan began historically in 1325." Depending on the various sources, scholars ascribe different dates for founding of Tenochtitlan.

altering and guiding the historical events of much of Mesoamerica.

For approximately a century after the founding of Tenochtitlan, the Mexica had been successful in overcoming in many impediments. The land they had settled was bordered by three powerful city states. In this circumstance, fearful of the future of their political status, they faced the problem of being tributaries of one of these powerful states. Although we can assume that the Mexica would have liked to maintain their independence, they chose a more pragmatic course and became subjects of the Tepanec city of Azcapotzalco. By around 1350, Azcapotzalco had achieved a bold military undertaking in the valley, conquering many cities and inflicting fear in the basin. These conquests did not always involve military confrontations; in some cases accommodations were made that recognized Azcapotzalco as the dominant power. In the Mexica case the latter applied. In a presumably wiser course, the Mexica agreed to provide tribute from the lake productions and in military service.

At the same time the Mexica sought to strengthen their position by looking for allies. Marriage provided a convenient means to create ties and ultimately establish alliances, and the Mexica rulers made a succession of shrewd marriages into long-established dynasties. Acamapichtli, the Mexica's first ruler, took a bride from the royal line of Culhuacan, hence establishing a close alliance with the Culhua. Acamapichtli's strategic marriage would later provide the future generations of Mexica rulers with a claim to Toltec heritage (Berden, 2005). As mentioned in the beginnings of this chapter, in the Valley of Mexico, descent from "ancient" Toltec nobility was viewed as legitimacy to rule.

Acamapichtli's son and successor, Huitzilihuitl, following in his father's footsteps created through marriage firm ties with the Tepanec ruler of Azcapotzalco, Tezozomoc. As a result of this latest marriage the relationship between Tenochtitlan and Azcapotzalco was further strengthened. The Tepanec rulers appeared to accommodate the Mexica, softening their tribute obligations and involving them in number of military conquests from witch the Mexica gained some territories. This favored position reflected itself in an eventual shift of power relations. According to Katz:

> In proportion to the rate at which the [Tepanec] conquests grew, the importance of the Aztec also increased. They were treated less and less as ordinary vassals and mercenaries and more and more as allies. A number of regions which they had conquered for Atzcapotzalco were made over to them and from there they obtained the timber which they lacked and a constantly increasing supply of food.

As their strength increased their influence in the making of political decisions seems also to have risen (Katz, 1972 p. 138).

Smith (1986) gives us another specific example of the influence of the practice of the Mexica's strategy of intermarriages with the region's stronger states. The example involves the alliance between the state of Cuauhnahuac and the Mexica through marriage between two royal dynasties around 1395, when Huitzilihuitl, the second Mexica tlatoani married Miahuaxlhuitle, the daughter of the Cuauhnahuac tlatoani. This was not the only marriage alliance; rather there were considerable intermarriages between Mexica and Cuauhnahuac royal families (See figure 3.5). Because of these intermarriages the Cuauhnahuac state looked at the Mexica in a favorable way, just as in the case of Tepanec state. In 1423, when the Cuauhnahuac attacked and conquered the Cohuixca area, they permitted the weaker rulers of Tenochtitlan and Tlatelolco to participate in the war effort and to share the victory, thus providing another example of inter-elite cooperation resulting from intermarriages between them (Smith, 1986 p. 79).

Further according to Smith:

The conquest of the Cohuisca [Cohuixca] was not accomplished by Mexica; the rulers of Quauhnauac

[Cuauhnahuac] only permitted them to participate in the conquest. The spoils of victory were shared with Tlacateutzin, ruler of Tlatelolco and Chiamlpopocatzin [third tlatoani] of Tenochtitlan (Smith, 1986 p. 79).

Just fifteen years after this episode, in 1438, the relative positions of Cuauhnahuac and Tenochtitlan were reversed, when the Mexica with their allies defeated the Cuauhnahuac in battle. By the time of the conquest of the Cuauhnahuac, the Mexica and their allies had considerably expanded their territories. The former Tepanec territories in western Morelos and the earlier independent states of Mazatepec, Zacatepec, and Xochitepec were all part of the Cuauhnahuac conquest in 1438 (Smith, 1983 pp. 104-109).

At this juncture, the Mexica population had rapidly outgrown the tiny island. This growth was a result of both natural increases and a sizable amount of immigration. This expanded population was settled into four divided quarters. Each quarter subsequently was divided into the smaller territories called calpulli already alluded to in the section above. Sometime at this point some of the elders and their followers were apparently displeased with this new arrangement and decided to leave the city. They chose Tlatelolco, a small island to the north of

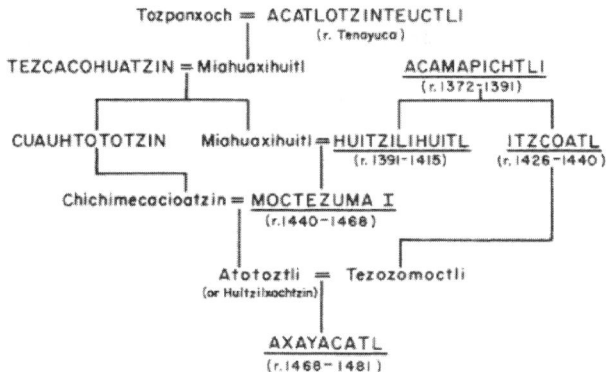

Figure 3.5 Intermarriages between Cuauhnahuac and Tenochtitlan ruling families. Names of tlatoque [tlatoani] are capitalized; Tenochtitlan tlatoque [tlatoani] are also underlined. The marriages taken from Nazareo and others (1941, p. 122); dates were those of Davies (1973, p. 305). Figure and caption source: (Smith, 1986 p. 78)

Tenochtitlan. Tlatelolco quickly became a considerably powerful commercial center, gradually becoming the largest and most active marketplace in the Valley of Mexico. (Tlatelolco was later conquered by the Mexica of Tenochtitlan in 1473).

The Mexica had taken full advantage of the time they had spent under Tepanec domination. Under the Tepanec rule the Mexica developed a strong and effective military force. In 1428 this strong military force, allied with neighboring Texcoco, ultimately turned against the Tepanec empire of Azcapotzalco. The allied forces of Tenochtitlan, Texcoco, and Tlacopan succeeded in crushing Tepanec in 1430. Success of this magnitude would be unseen in the future history of Mesoamerica, a future that was dominated by the Mexica and their two allies. For the next 90 years this Triple Alliance engaged in a course of military expansion unprecedented in the history of Mesoamerica (Berden, 2005).

However, all was not well within the Alliance, known as the Aztec empire. Rivalries threatened to tear it apart, until one city, Tenochtitlan rose above the others. Despite the name Triple Alliance, Tenochtitlan was the dominant partner, and Tlacopan the weakest. By the time the Spanish arrived in 1520, Tlacopan had nearly disappeared as a separate city-state, and the lands of the Alliance were ruled from Tenochtitlan (Berdan, 2005 p. 110; Townsend, 1992 p.64 and p. 72).

Furthermore, according to Elizabeth H. Boone and Tom Commins:

> In 1520, when Fernando Cortés recorded in his "Second Letter" to the king of Spain what had transpired during his *entrada* of the previous year, he stated that a single powerful ruler governed most of the territory from the Gulf coast to the central highlands. That ruler was known as Moctezuma

(the Hispanicized form of Moteuczoma), and he ruled from the city of "Temixtitan" (Tenochtitlan) located in "Mesyco." His kingdom, founded on the conquest or forced incorporation of other polities, was known as "Culua" (Colhua) (Cortés 1971, pp. 50, 74). As Cortés (1971, p. 173) explained, ". . . the name Culua comprises all the lands and provinces in this region subject to Temixtitan [Tenochtitlan]." Thus Cortés, writing before the conquest, observed that Moctezuma, ruler of Tenochtitlan, was the supreme head of the "Culua empire," which later become known as the Aztec empire (Boone and Commins, 1998, p. 237).

In the context of this research endeavor the superiority and the ascendance of Tenochtitlan within the Triple Alliance (Aztec empire) is very important. This research effort will mainly concentrate on Tenochtitlan, the political, economic, as well as the cultural center of the Aztec empire. From the importance of the role of chinampas in Tenochtitlan this research will infer the importance of the chinampas in Aztec empire.

The process of the birth of Aztec Empire, which began in the 15th and 16th centuries continuously expanded and became the most powerful entity in the entire history of Mesoamerica. Only the arrival of the Spaniards would topple this legendary empire. However the effects of the Aztec empire can readily be seen in today's Mexican psyche, culture, and society.

CHAPTER 4

The Role of Chinampas in Aztec State Formation

A state is seen as powerful, complex, semi-permanently instituted system of centralized political administration. Emanating from these characteristics, a state has the power to exercise sovereignty in carrying out tasks such as maintaining territorial rights, internal order, making and discharging decisions regarding group action. A state's authority in these matters is reinforced by its ability in the use of force within its jurisdiction (Keesing, 1976 p. 348; Yoffee, 1979 pp. 14-17 as cited in Brumfiel, 1983 p. 261). A state is distinguished by administrative complexity and its bureaucratic personnel, hierarchically ordered and specialized by administrative tasks (Wright, 1978 pp. 49-68 as cited in Brumfiel, 1983 p. 261).

Aztec state formation was a result of interplay between small but autonomous city states within the geographical confines of the Valley of Mexico and the immediate adjacent areas. The formation of the Triple Alliance hastened the course towards the consolidation of political authority on the regional level. Hence, the period of Triple Alliance formation is classified as the beginning of Aztec state creation (Brumfiel, 1983 pp. 266-268).

Theoretical Considerations

There have been numerous attempts to explain the reason behind formation of states in some places but not in others. These attempts have been dominated by two contrasting approaches: the ecological and the structural. The ecological approach is based on the work of Julian H. Steward (1949), who relates state creation to the obstacles and/or conveniences available in a human population by its environmental peculiarities. The central theme of this approach is the population growth with its resulting pressures, which creates certain dynamics prone to state formation. It is in this dynamic, at least in the initial stages of state formation, that the state's major role is to promote ecological benefits to its general population. Thus, the ecology, or the relationships between organisms and their environments, becomes a catalyst in at least the first stage of state formation.

The second major approach, the structural approach, grew out of the Marxist tradition, and regards state formation as a process generated by specific sociocultural orders. The structural approach focuses on the internal dynamics of certain types of societies that bring on pressure and cause the formation of states, regardless of the environmental and ecological effects on the societies. This approach tends to delegate more importance to the social components and their structures, rather than the population of the society as a whole. The ecological approach has received more attention by the researchers in their quest to analyze state formation, while the structural approach has been less thoroughly explored (Brumfiel, 1983).

The scope and the aim of this study is not to analyze the differences or the superiority either one of these approaches in explaining state formation; rather the main focus of this chapter is to examine the creation of the Aztec state through both approaches and to find evidence in explaining the importance of the role of chinampa agriculture in the formation of the Aztec state. Before that however, it is useful to explain and revisit the concept that by Aztec state we should understand a confederation of independent city states of Tenochtitlan, Tetzcoco, and Tlacopan, each with its own tributary domain (Refer to chapter 3). Nevertheless this confederation can also be seen as a state, in that the actions of these separate entities were coordinated and, although separate in their market exchange, were fully integrated and they formed a single region-wide system.

The Role of Chinampas in Aztec State Formation through the Lens of the Ecological Approach

By its nature, the state is a capable, specialized entity for political administration. Hence, a state can function as a decidedly effective problem solver. State agents can use their position to gather information regarding the problems that are faced by the society. They become experts in problem solving, and they can use their position to gather information concerning the problems. They can also mobilize the manpower and materials needed to solve those problems. Recognition of this ability of the state effectively to manage environmental resources is a major insight provided by the ecological approach. It is also the basis from which the ecological hypothesis of state formation is developed. The hypothesis asserts that states arise in a socio-environmental context where effective management is either necessary or particularly beneficial. According to Brumfiel (1983), this hypothesis has so far proven to be enduring.

Initially, however, scholars such as Julian H. Steward (1949) and Karl A. Wittfogel (1957) assumed that early states were a reaction to the managerial dilemmas of constructing and preserving large-scale irrigation. This argument is no longer universally credible, since archeological findings have exposed cases in which states emerged in the absence of large-scale irrigation

(Adams, 1960 p. 281). Regardless, problem solving is a major role of the state; hence many versions of the managerial hypothesis have surfaced by experts on the process of state formation. Sanders (1956, and 1968 as cited in Brumfiel, 1983 p. 262), for example, promotes the view that states form to facilitate internal distribution of wealth. (Hole, 1966 and Rathje, 1971 as cited in Brumfiel, 1983 p. 262) argue that states form to acquire vital raw materials from outside their domain. Sanders and Price (1968 as cited in Brumfiel, 1983 p. 262) argue for the importance of state formation for the purpose of defending the resources of population or capturing the resources of others. Athens (1977 as cited in Brumfiel, 1983 p. 262) assigns the reason for state formation to stabilization of agricultural productivity. Thus, we see that the emphasis on the managerial performance of the states has given ecological approach an enormously effective tool to deal with various sets of specific cases with a single, broad descriptive theorem.

Looking through the lens of the ecological approach, we can find numerous reasons for the importance of the chinampa agricultural system in Aztec state formation. Let us examine this issue by looking at various managerial functions of the state as the cause of state creation, mentioned above.

The Aztec State and Internal Distribution of Wealth

At the beginning of the Aztec settlement in the Valley of Mexico, the Aztecs were a relatively un-stratified group. The social structure was composed of a loose association of lineage heads. However, as they progressed in terms of state formation, the Aztecs created nobility composed of the lineage heads through their intermarriage with offspring of the kings of allied city states who were allegedly descended from Toltecs (See chapter 3). As the nobility gradually took hold, the socioeconomic disparity among the Aztecs grew. The chinampa agricultural system was the main basis for the wealth of Aztec nobility, which initially came from the growing calpullis that had gradually extended and acquired vast chinampa fields, hence producing surpluses that could be channeled through taxes to the nobility. In some cases the nobility themselves owned vast chinampa lands themselves.

Therefore the chinampa farming system was essential in creating a more stratified socioeconomic society in the Aztec state formation process. Without chinampas, there could not have been an expansion of calpullis, and with no calpullis there could not have been a base for stratification of the society on socioeconomic terms. The nobles' base of wealth was either the direct ownership of a vast amount of chinampa lands or income from the lands owned by the calpullis. The members of the calpullis themselves also expanded their wealth through the expansion of their chinampa holdings.

At the later stage of state development the calpullis would gradually loose their role as the main source of wealth for the nobles (Townsend, 1992). However, chinampas would always remain as the basis of the nobles' as well as the calpulli members' wealth. Here there can be an argument that the nobles' wealth came from tributes as opposed to agricultural products from their chinampa field holdings and income from the lands owned by the calpullis. We should keep in mind though that the tributes were composed of mainly agricultural goods produced in chinampa fields, especially in the beginning stages of state formation. Cook (1947 p. 50) estimates that even during the latest stage of the Aztec state formation the tributes were composed of 1/3 agricultural goods from chinampas, the rest being men for the war effort, raw materials, and, in the later stage of the Aztec empire, luxury goods.

Hence, the chinampas were essential and played a major role in creating the wealth of the Aztec society and its distribution among the elements of the society. By extension, we should conclude that the chinampas were essential and had a major role in internal distribution of wealth as a function of Aztec state formation.

The Aztec State and Procuring Essential Extra-local Raw Materials

The Aztec state formation was, looking through the lens of the ecological approach, in part due to procuring extra-local raw materials, which included timber and other building materials for the construction of their cities, but more importantly, it was needed to procure suitable locations for expanding the chinampa agriculture. The Valley of Mexico accommodated the necessary environment for the Aztecs to settle and prosper. During the Aztec empire (1428-1521), the landscape looked like a bowel filed with water, with five lakes, surrounded by mountain ranges. "This physical geography provided the raw materials for the Mexica to build the Aztec Empire." (Aguilar, 2006 p. 56). However, obtaining the suitable fields of this physical geography, mainly to use for chinampa agriculture, seems to account for a major part of Aztec state formation. The state formation was essential to procure the raw materials for their building from the neighboring city states, in majority of the cases through warfare, especially in the later phase of Aztec state formation. The first Aztec buildings were simple structures of fibers and reeds. Eventually though temples were built and were rebuilt, growing into magnificent temples such as the temple of Huitzilopochtli (Hagen, 1962 p. 129).

However, an important condition that fostered this warfare was the agricultural fertility of the neighboring city states. And it was due mostly to these fertile chinampa agricultural fields that Aztecs started and expanded their conquest of neighboring city states. Because of the productivity of the chinampa system, Smith (1992, p. 85), argues that:

> ...the result was that comparatively little labor was needed to produce enough food to live on... Part of the resulting crop surpluses went to feed the cities in the form of tribute; but a labor surplus remained, leaving men able to pursue militaristic ambitions. One effect was to produce a hierarchical social structure, in which different groups of people emerged, such as warrior and priestly class.

This assertion also goes to support the argument that the Aztec state formation was in part, through developing and conquering chinampa fields, responsible for stratification of the society and internal distribution of wealth, one of the arguments of the structural approach to state formation (to be discussed later in the chapter).

Hence, we again encounter an important contribution of the chinampa farming system. In this case, the important role that it played in creating the surplus for the Aztec state; deductively it helped the war effort needed for procuring essential extra-local raw materials.

The Aztec State and Defending the Resources of the Population or Capturing the Resources of Others

The Valley of Mexico is distinguished by the limitation of arable land. The arable lands were limited to areas around the lake system and parts of the fresh water lakes suitable for chinampa cultivation (Evans, 1980). The role played by the Aztec state in defending these regions was a major factor in developing and maintaining the chinampa system. On the other hand, since the neighboring city states had more suitable chinampa lands, one of the Aztec state's major roles became to capture those resources from neighboring city states, particularly the region of Xochimilco, which because of the lack of salinity in its lake shores had the most suitable land for chinampa farming, with already developed and long standing chinampa agriculture. The Aztec state would later further develop the chinampa system in the Xochimilco region at a rate never seen before in the Valley of Mexico or anywhere else for that matter. According to Aguilar (2006), the chinampa agricultural zone in the Xochimilco region produced about half of the food for Tenochtitlan, which at that juncture may have had as many as 150,000 inhabitants.

Tenochas (inhabitants of Tenochtitlan), in other words the Aztecs, perpetually needed new tracts of lands suitable for chinampa agriculture in order to sustain themselves. The Aztec state accomplished this by annexing most of the city states in the Valley of Mexico. They used the conquered population to build, develop, and augment aqueducts and chinampa fields. Every aspect of maintenance, from irrigation to fertilization, was centrally administered and managed by the Aztec state. Aguilar (2006 p. 58) notes that "The Aztec were so concerned about not letting anything go to waste, that the chinampa gardens were even fertilized with human excrement collected in canoes from Tenochtitlan and then transported to the fields."

Parsons and others (1982) posit that the success of the Aztecs in terms of state building was mainly a product of the key role of the Chalco-Xochimilco region in catering to the large urban center of Tenochtitlan. "The impressive expansion of chinampa cultivation over most of the lake Chalco-Xochimilco was one response to the need to secure this food supply [for Tenochtitlan population]." (Parsons et al., 1982 pp. 383-384).

From the evidence above, we can infer the very important role of the chinampa farming system in the Aztecs' life in general. In this case particularly we can conclude that one of the functions of the

Aztec state and part of the reason for Aztec state formation was to defend its own resources and to capture the resources of others, which were needed for their subsistence at the beginning and later for further expansion of their influence and rule across the Valley of Mexico and beyond.

The Aztec State and Stabilizing Agricultural Productivity

Sanders, Parsons, and Santley (1979 pp. 222 – 281) and Rojas Rabiela (1985) cited in Smith and Price, 1994 p. 169) propose that the Aztecs employed three types of agricultural methods to provide sustenance for their densely populated urban centers. These were canal irrigation, chinampas, and terracing. However, the terrace agricultural system was not as productive as the other two types, and it expanded later in limited areas when the Aztecs were already established as an empire. Canal irrigation is closely related to chinampa agriculture, and I do not agree in differentiating the two for purpose of this particular investigation. Hence, chinampa remains the method of Aztec's agricultural practice. Thus, investigating about the Aztec state and stabilizing agricultural productivity, this project will focus mainly on chinampa agriculture and its productivity. This is not to dismiss canal irrigation and the terracing method, but as mentioned above, for the particular purpose at hand the terracing method has little consequence and the canal irrigation is closely connected to chinampa agriculture and was developed in later stages of Aztec empire, rather than during the Aztec state formation about which this investigation is concerned.

According to Parsons (1976), most of the chinampa fields were created by direct Aztec state intervention. Additionally, there was apparatus created by the Aztec state such as massive systems of dams, sluice gates, and canals in order to regulate the water level that made the continued operation and maintenance of the chinampa system possible. An example of this kind of massive undertaking was evident in the entire Chalco-Xochimilco lake bed (Blanton, 1972 pp. 172-173; Palerm, 1955 pp. 36-38 as cited in Parsons, 1976, p. 253).

Furthermore, Parsons asserts that:

> Given the critical significance of the state presence in chinampa operation, the apparent intensity of chinampa cultivation may reflect the concern of the Aztec state with insuring an adequate subsistence base for its principal urban center. Because most chinampa cultivation of fifteenth and sixteenth centuries could not function without direct state management of critical water-control apparatus, the

state probably could have issued directives concerning productivity and disposition of produce with reasonable assurance that such directives would be followed (Parsons, 1976 pp. 253-254).

Parsons' (1976) investigation reveals a crucial role of the Aztec state in managing the chinampa agricultural system during the fifteenth and sixteenth centuries. From this work we can reasonably deduce that the Aztec state's management of chinampas did not occur suddenly in a vacuum; rather it was a gradual process that started from the beginning of Aztec state formation. That takes us back to formation of the Triple Alliance and even further back to the era in which Tenochtitlan was expanding rapidly in terms of population growth and the calpullis' development of new chinampa fields. Thus, it is logical to assume that chinampas must have played a major role in the development of antecedents required for the conception of the Aztec state, since it was one of the most vital preconditions of the Aztecs' (earlier the Mexica) growth, even before the creation of alliances with neighboring city states and the later conquest of them through warfare. Furthermore, we can reasonably conclude that one of the important roles of the Aztec state was to establish agricultural productivity through the chinampa agricultural system, hence revealing the importance of chinampas in Aztec state creation and, even more importantly, the subsequent vital role of chinampas in Aztec empire building and its expansion.

Other Considerations of Chinampas under the Ecological Approach to Aztec State Formation

Another major factor in the explanation of state creation through the ecological approach is population growth and the need for a mechanism or an entity to manage the growth and to create social order. According to Brumfiel (1983 p. 277), the overall agricultural productivity of the Valley of Mexico, which was represented mostly by the chinampa agricultural system, was critical in sustaining sufficient population, and it enabled Triple Alliance rulers to engage in public works through which they expanded and strengthened the Aztec state. The advancement of new chinampa agricultural fields and the importation of foodstuffs to the valley in the form of tribute assessments, which again were mainly was cultivated through chinampa system, supported the population growth. According to Sanders, Parsons, and Stanley (1979 pp. 183-184 as cited in Brumfiel, 1983 p. 277), by the time of the Spaniards' arrival, the population of the Valley of Mexico was about four times that of any earlier era in prehistoric epoch. Elizabeth Brumfiel writes,

> Population growth and its ensuing problems would explain why, after centuries without the benefits of state organization, a human population might suddenly find a state system either beneficial or necessary (Steward 1949: 19; Sanders and Price 1968: 230; Carneiro 1970: 735-736; kottak 1972: 368; Logan and Sanders 1976: 38; Athens 1977: 366; Santley 1980: 141). States would emerge only in certain environmental settings: where the problems of population growth were particularly severe because growth rate was high or arable land limited or where overpopulation could be accommodated by the application of some managerial strategy (construction of irrigation systems or other means of agricultural intensification, administration of local exchange systems or long distance trade, etc.) (1983, p. 262).

Taking population growth as the unit of analysis through the ecological model, we easily can connect the population growth in Aztec society to the existence and productivity of chinampa agriculture.

Parsons (1976), Cook (1947), Armillas (1971), and others clearly have shown the correlation between the population growth and the chinampa agricultural system. There can be little doubt of the chinampas' role in stimulating the Aztec population growth; and if we accept the ecological approach's claim as to the formation of a state due to population growth, then we have clearly shown the immensely important role that the chinampa agricultural system played in Aztec state formation and by extension in the Aztec empire building and its expansion.

It is almost certain that the Aztec state performed many of the ecological functions that the proponents of the ecological approach would expect of such a powerful, bureaucratic political state. Clearly then, the ecological variables are greatly implicated in the process of Aztec state formation. This conclusion has been reached by many researchers, (for example Armillas, 1964; Brumfiel, 1983), and the present study, with special attention to chinampa agricultural system as the main ecological variable, confirms their findings.

The hope is that by now it is clear that the chinampa agricultural system was a major component of the Aztec ecology, and as such, it was one of the ecological variables most responsible in affecting the Aztec state formation. It seems inconceivable to think of the ecology of the valley of Mexico without the chinampa system of agriculture.

The relationship between the chinampa agricultural system and the Aztec state was not only based on the supply of the foodstuff needs, but also transportation and by extension the commercial endeavors as well. The chinampa agricultural system produced food, but it also created a means of convenient transportation through its canals, which were essential for transportation of goods in the absence of effective roadways and wheels. Those researchers who concentrate on the tribute system and commerce as the key factors for the Aztec state building and expansion seem to take the transportation ability of the Aztecs for granted. Without the existence of the transportation means, which was mostly due to the canals created by the ingenious chinampa farming system, there could not have been a viable way to collect tribute or to engage in commercial activities.

Most of the researchers adhering to the ecological approach have relied on population growth and constant population pressure with limited resources to explain state formation. However, according to several sources provided by Brumfiel (1983 p. 263), there are many cases in which states have appeared in the absence of population pressures. This being the case, other researchers such as Yoffee (1979, pp. 26-27 as cited in Brumfiel, 1983 p. 263) have proposed that we observe causes of state formation within state structure itself.

The Role of Chinampas in Aztec State Formation through the Lens of Structural Approach

The phrase structural approach arose from the assertions of a number of anthropologists who attributed the dynamic nature of some sociocultural systems to their inherent structural properties. Elman R. Service (1975, p. 358 as cited in Brumfiel 1983, p. 263) describes the advancement of the state and civilization as being "orthogenetic" and "self-contained". J. Friedman and M. J. Rowland "speak in terms of 'epigenesis': structural transformation over time in which the trajectory of change is determined by structural properties of the initial system" (1978 p. 204 as cited in Brumfiel 1983 p. 263). It was this approach that Brumfiel (1983, p. 261) designated as the structural approach to state formation.

Frederic Engels (1972 [1884] as cited in Brumfiel 1983, p. 263) was responsible for the first conflict theory of state formation. Explaining Marx's ideas, Engels wrote that the state formed when new industrial techniques, such as "cattle raising, loom weaving, forging metal tools", created various economic institution such as "private property, money lending at interest, mercantile exchange, and the use of slave labor", by which the society divided into a number of strata, each with conflicting "mutually antagonistic" economic interests. The formation of the state was as a result of evolution of a mechanism that could advance internal order and mediate between those "mutually antagonistic" social classes and ultimately suppress those conflicts. Although most scholars disagree with Engle's assertion that state formation was simply as a direct result of some technological advancement, the evidence for private property, mercantile exchange, and slave labor among early states has led some modern scholars to accept conflicts of economic interest as a potential cause of state formation (Brumfiel, 1983 p. 263), thus, suggesting that the state results from particular sociocultural orders, while the relationship between the environment and population, pivotal in the case of the environmental approach, is seen as relatively stable.

The Role of Chinampas in Sociocultural Orders in Aztec Society

To establish the importance of the role of the chinampa in Aztec state creation through the structural approach, this part of the investigation shall attempt to examine the Aztecs' sociocultural orders during and before the creation of the Aztec state. To achieve this aim the paper shall embark on finding the effects and the role of the chinampa agricultural system in the Aztec sociocultural orders, thereby establishing the important role that chinampa agriculture played in Aztec state formation through the structural approach to state formation.

Looking back to the era of tribal migration to the valley of Mexico, the departure of the tribes from their ancestral lands was part of a celestial command instructing all tribes to abandon their original caves and find "places of pleasant weather" and "agricultural abundance." The tribal departure from the caves was gradual. Some groups left earlier and some waited for a specific celestial sign in order to leave. "This passive and lengthy abandonment of Aztec/Chicomoztoc allows room to speculate that besides agricultural or climatic reasons that forced the massive migration, it could have been also motivated by philosophical or religious beliefs." (Aguilar, 2006, p. 31).

This is important in terms of the structural approach, since there is an argument here that there was something other than agricultural, or in general, environmental reasons for the tribal migration. That something was part of the sociocultural beliefs of the tribes that is worth investigating, if we are approaching the Aztec state formation though the structural model of state formation.

Part of these philosophical beliefs included the belief that the Mexica tribe considered themselves as chosen people by their supreme deity, Huitzilopochtli. Aguilar (2006, p. 32), writes that the Mexica, the last tribe to leave the seven caves (their original habitats), adopted their name to honor their high priest *Mexitl*, who led the migration presumably by the order of their supreme deity Huitzilopochtli. Huitzilopochtli favored the Mexica above the other original tribes and had reserved a land of abundance for them.

This philosophical and religious belief is an important variable of the sociocultural order of the Mexica, later Aztecs, which may have had a determining effect on the Mexica in their resoluteness and hardiness that, in the long run, made them the masters of the Valley of Mexico, by enduring the many hardships in the process (refer to chapter 3). Once they chose to settle in their permanent uninhabited place, they had to overcome several obstacles gradually to turn themselves into the undisputed political and cultural center of the Aztec empire with their city, Tenochtitlan, as the center. As mentioned earlier in chapter three, one of the first endeavors that occupied the Mexica in their new found permanent home was the creation and development of the chinampa agricultural plots for their immediate sustenance needs. Building chinampas was labor intensive and required a determined group of people with strong sociocultural bonds to succeed in the endeavor. It is very easily conceivable to consider that the Mexica's philosophical and religious views of seeing themselves as the chosen people along with their then democratic political structure (both, part of their sociocultural order) gave them the will power and necessary context in which to engage in such a crucial as well as difficult task of creating and developing the chinampa fields.

At the time the political and sociocultural structure of the Mexica was not particularly stratified. At the center of the political and sociocultural structure was the institution of the calpulli. We have already described the calpulli in an earlier chapter. Here we revisit calpulli in the context of the Mexica political and sociocultural structure to align our research with that of the structural approach to state formation. The calpulli was the basic unit of social membership in early Mexica society. In addition to its economic and organizational functions, the calpulli was a type of kinship structure. According to Geoffrey W. Conrad and Arthur A. Demarest (1984, p. 24),

> Early Mexica leadership roles, like the class differences were far less sharply ranked than they would become in the imperial period. Most accounts portray early Mexica society as possessing considerable democratic qualities, with the calpulli leaders being elected by the general membership of commoners (macehualtin) and advised by a council of elders.

Thus, the democratic nature of the Mexica political and sociocultural structure at the time allowed for or assisted in development of their subsistence base through their engagement in developing chinampa agricultural plots. The democratic nature of the Mexica political and sociocultural structure and the fact that the society was less stratified at the time than later may also explain the advantage of Mexica in warfare as well. According to Christopher Chase-Dunn (1991, p. 102),

> Citizen solders who believed they had a stake in the collectivity are better warriors than conscripted peasants or paid mercenaries, as such a belief is easier to sustain when the differences between nobles and commoners are less extreme.

Later the Aztecs would become more stratified within as they expanded their power base in the Valley of Mexico. After the conquering of other tribes and the forming of the Triple Alliance, the Aztec state through acquisition of tributes made the nobles wealthier and caused a more stratified political and sociocultural structure. The fundamental division at that point in terms of political and sociocultural structure was the division between the nobility and the commoners. The distinction between nobility and commoners was established by birth. With the practice of intermarriages, discussed earlier, and the widespread practice of "polygyny" among nobles, and the fact that nobility status was traditionally transmitted through either male or female links, the nobility may have "numbered in tens of thousand by the early sixteenth century" (Calnek, 1974 p. 202). But until the deepening of the stratification of political and sociocultural structures in Aztec society, the role and importance of chinampas became even more profound as the Mexica's main objective became to conquer the neighboring chinampa fields. This ultimately led to the state formation and empire building and expansionism through the chinampa's role of sustaining the primary needs of the society.

According to Brian Fagan (1984, p.61),

> From the very beginning, the Mexica rulers realized that control of good agricultural land, not long distance trade, war, or religious prestige, must be their primary power base. Their long term political objective was simple: to acquire land, land, and still more land.

Later, when the maintenance and the expansion of the chinampa agricultural system became a centralized operation by the already well established Aztec state, for example through expansion of irrigation channels, creating dams, sluice gates, etc., the chinampas played both economic as well as social roles in the development of Aztec civilization. Thus the structure of the Aztec society and the chinampa system were mutually interconnected. The sociocultural order of the Aztecs, as discussed above, helped in creating and expanding the chinampa agricultural system. In turn the chinampa system created an environment in which the sociocultural order of the Aztec state became a dynamic process of change. Partly because of the productivity and wealth created by chinampas, Aztec society became more stratified in terms of class structures through the nobility, who acquired their position both through lineages as well as the income generated mainly by the surplus production of the chinampas.

One of the main components of the sociocultural order of Aztec society was their religious beliefs. In the context of the structural approach to state formation, it is useful to consider the Aztec religion and its role in their sociocultural order, as well as its potential role in Aztec state formation through the chinampa agricultural system. There are numerous works on the Aztec religion, encompassing every aspect of the Aztec life. For the purpose at hand, I will concentrate on the Aztec religious beliefs as they relate to agriculture, in the hope of explaining their effect as part of the overall role of the sociocultural order in Aztec state formation.

The Aztec society was essentially an agricultural one. For the Aztecs the rainy season and other environmentally related phenomena that influenced their crops were fundamentally very important. Thus, it seems natural that they would worship gods of weather, water, and of vegetation, placing them in the central part of their religious life. *Tlaloc*, "he who makes things grow", god of the rain and of lightening was one of the most influential deities in the Aztec religion (Caso, 1978 p. 41). *Chicomecoatl*, "Seven Serpent," was the most important of the many gods of vegetation (Caso, 1978 p. 45). They were even favorite gods worshiped by chinamperos. *Xochipilli*, "the prince of flowers", and *Xochiquetzal*, "the flower of the rich plume", were worshiped mainly by chinamperos (Caso, 1978 p. 47). The mere existence of several gods for agricultural, and even specific gods worshiped by chinamperos, leads us to conclude that agriculture in general and chinampa the farming system in particular played a major role in Aztec sociocultural order. Therefore, agriculture and the chinampas in particular must have had a major impact on the structure of Aztec society, leading us to conclude that chinampas must have played a major role in Aztec state formation by virtue of their influence as being a major part of the sociocultural order in Aztec society.

Although in the case of Aztec state formation, in the context of the role of chinampa agricultural system, the ecological approach seems to be a more useful approach, the structural model can also provide its share of input in contributing to an understanding of the importance of the role of chinampas in Aztec state formation. This part of the research clearly is not an in-depth exercise in describing Aztec state formation through the structural approach. Rather, in the context of this study, it has been a general consideration of the chinampa agricultural system and its role in Aztec state creation through the structural approach. As such this section is far from being a thorough study of Aztec state formation through the lens of the structural approach. This is yet another interesting topic that needs further specialized investigation.

CHAPTER 5

The Role of Chinampas in Aztec Empire Expansion

It would be logical to write about the transition from Aztec state to Aztec empire at this time since this chapter deals with Aztec empire and the importance of the role of chinampas in its creation and expansion. However, since I have already described the process of Aztec empire creation in chapter three (the historical background) I will only briefly refer to it here. The reader will remember that the Aztec empire, as it is known today, was formed through the Triple Alliance of three powerful city states of Tenochtitlan, Texcoco, and Tlacopan when the alliance threw off the Atzcapotzalco yoke in 1430 and established their dominance in the Valley of Mexico. It is also very important to remember Tenochtitlan's central role in Aztec empire, especially during the expansion of the Aztec empire. In the attempt to establish the importance of the role of chinampas in Aztec empire-building and expansion, this research will mainly focus on the important role of chinampas in Tenochtitlan, and infer from that the importance of the chinampas in Aztec empire-building and expansion, since the Tenochtitlan was indisputably the hub of the Aztec empire. The head of the Spanish conquerors, Cortes witnessed and wrote (see chapter 3, pp. 46-47) that Tenochtitlan was the supreme head of the Aztec empire.

In the previous chapter this research endeavor has attempted to establish the role of the chinampa agricultural system in Aztec state creation. Some of the arguments introduced in previous the chapter regarding the role of chinampas in Aztec state formation overlap with the arguments regarding the role of chinampas in the Aztec empire expansion as well. (See for example pages 59-60 and 62 of chapter four). Nevertheless, in this chapter, the specific issue at hand is the role of chinampa agriculture system in the period of expansion of Aztec empire. Therefore, I will mainly concentrate on the period of the fifteenth and the early sixteenth centuries when the Aztecs, having established their state, had moved on to become an ever expanding empire.

To establish the importance of the chinampa agricultural system in Aztec empire expansionary period, I will primarily rely on the sources that can provide evidence of the systematic efforts of the Aztecs in this period to expand the chinampa agricultural system. The Aztec undertaking of massive and centralized projects to expand the chinampas, through various means to be discussed in this chapter, indicates the important role that the Aztecs attributed to the chinampas, at the least in providing sustenance for their ever growing population in their urban centers and for the maintenance of their status as an empire as well as their expansionist policies. By insuring their sustenance base through the chinampa agricultural system the Aztecs were free and able to engage in their expansionist policies, though wars and at times through mere threat of wars.

Expansion of Chinampas through the Irrigation System

The chinampa agricultural system had a vital role in Aztecs' sustenance, and in turn it played a major role in maintaining and expanding the Aztec empire. The Aztecs canalized rivers and created artificial sweet water lagoons to increase the area of chinampa cultivation. They controlled the water level and salinity of the water, both necessary for cultivation of chinampas, through a multiplicity of causeway-dikes, which divided the lakes into compartments.

Sluyter (1994) discusses what he calls intensive wetland agriculture in Mesoamerica. "Intensive wetland agriculture goes by various names: raised fields, ridged fields, ditched fields, camellones, platform fields, chinampas…" (Sluyter, 1994 p. 557). According to Sluyter, chinampas, the prominent wetland fields in the Xochimilco-Chalco sub-basin, have been the focus of attention for earlier researchers. Sluyter continues that:

> Since the 1940's when investigators began to apply techniques to estimate chronologies and hectareages (Armillas 1971, Avila Lopez 1991; Serra Puche 1988; West and Armillas 1950), research has accented the role of chinampas as the subsistence base for the Aztec and, perhaps, Teotihuacan states… (Sluyter, 1994 p. 560).

Here, Sluyter (1994) has provided this research a source that directly attests to the importance of the chinampas in their role of being the subsistence base for the Aztecs, hence affirming the viability of the hypothesis of this research.

Armillas' (1971) investigation and survey based on the interpretation of aerial photographs and the inspection of grounds of old chinampa fields is a rich source for establishing the Aztecs' effort in chinampa expansion during the empire expansion. Armillas' survey reveals that the extent of the raised chinampa plots in the Xochimilco-Chalco Basin was much greater in the Aztec period than had been earlier recognized. The archeological evidence gathered by this survey has also been substantiated by the descriptions left by 16th century witnesses of native land reclamation methods (Armillas, 1971 p. 659).

Sanders and others (1979) wrote another comprehensive work, witch includes various surreys on the existence and the expansions of the chinampa fields in Mesoamerica, and as such it is an important source to establish the expansion of the chinampas in the Aztec empire period. According to Sanders, Parsons, and Stanley, the most industrious prehistoric project in Mesoamerica was created by the Aztecs within the confines of lake Chalco-Xochimilco. Before discussing this impressive project in the context of the role of chinampa agricultural system in Aztec empire expansion, it is useful to cite from Sanders (1965), which is meant to be direct evidence towards establishing the hypothesis of this research.

> This system, called chinampa cultivation, is probably the most intensive and productive kind of agriculture practiced in the New World in pre-Hispanic times... As the system was expanded, most of the surfaces of Lake Chalco-Xochimilco and Lake Mexico (part of Lake Texcoco diked off from the main lake) were reduced from open lake into a network of chinampas and canals. An added

advantage of this system is that produce could be loaded from chinampa into canoes, and poled directly to the urban markets, along the lakeshores or in towns within the lake, such as Aztec Tenochtitlan and colonial Mexico City. The growth of urban centers in and on the lakes in the Aztec period was, in part, correlated with the evolution of this system of agriculture (Sanders, 1965 p. 44).

Armillas (1971) maintains that chinampas were constructed by creating a large network of drainage ditches, which slowly reduced the water content of the soil making the cultivation of land possible. Armillas' survey data indicates that the progress of colonization started from islands and offshore areas on the mainland, rather than from within the lakes themselves. The ditches, which were used to drain the area, were also utilized as means of transportation. As did Sanders (1965), Armillas also maintains that the ditches facilitated the transportation of agricultural products. Later Aztecs constructed larger dikes to further regulate water distribution, most probably to restrict flooding during the rainy season. The extraordinary regularity of the chinampa plots is an indication of centralized planning (Armillas 1971).

Sanders and others (1979) suggest that the evidence from their and Armillas' (1971) surveys strongly indicates that the bulk of the chinampa system in the Chalco-Xochimilco lakebed areas was constructed and expanded during the late horizon period (1350-1521 C.E.), and that most probably these efforts to expand the chinampa system were planned by central governments within the Aztec empire. This may have been carried out either by local authorities of municipalities such as Tlahuac, Mixquic, or Xochimilco, but some of it may have been organized by the authorities of Tenochtitlan themselves (Sanders et al, 1979 p. 280). Either way both the local authorities and the authorities of Tenochtitlan were part of the Aztecs' political structure; thus we can confidently conclude that the Aztecs planned these expansions of chinampas through a central policy. Furthermore, it was because of chinampas that the Aztec empire could survive and perhaps even be strengthened and expand further. This is yet another good argument for the important role of chinampa agricultural system in Aztec empire expansion.

Sanders and others (1979) posit that because of the application of rich lakebed mud and vegetation the chinampas would have been elevated, reducing the danger of flooding. Considering the long amount of time that it takes for the vegetation to amass in the soil, the cross sections of chinampas suggest that they were constructed artificially.

Sanders and his fellow authors' (1979) survey had also found small localized areas of chinampas in lakes Texcoco and Xaltocan (in the community of Xaltocan). In those areas local springs provided enough fresh water to reduce the salinity of the areas. However, later in the early fifteenth century the Mexica of Tenochtitlan converted the western one third of Lake Texcoco into a fresh water lake, by construction of an elaborate network of dikes with sluice gates. The Mexica also brought fresh water from nearby mountains into the basin, thus converting the area's saline waters into fresh water, rapidly. This created the suitable infrastructure for expansion of even more chinampa construction and cultivation[10] (Sanders et al, 1979 p. 281).

Sanders and his fellow authors continue that from the early horizon period (1400 C.E. - 400 B.C.E.) until the late horizon (1350-1521 C.E.), their settlement surveys indicate the existence of nucleated settlements sustained by chinampa agriculture in the immediate lake shores and on peninsulas and islands within the lake. Regardless of the possibility of existence of chinampa cultivation in earlier times, both "Armillas' [Armillas, 1971] surveys and our own, clearly demonstrate that there was a rapid, planned, massive colonization of the lakebed during the fifteenth century." (Sanders et al, 1979 p. 281). They

---

[10] For considerable more details on construction of this system see Palerm, (1973).

explain that the conclusion is based on the number and the regularity of canal systems, which show an involvement of highly planned irrigation of natural waterways with a network of artificially created ditches of different size, indicating a centralized planning scheme (Sanders et al, 1979 p. 281).

Townsend (1992) has suggested three major factors in explanation of the Aztec empire building process. First, he considers the location of the island of Tenochtitlan as favorable. He suggests that Tenochtitlan "the unclaimed outcrops and reedbeds proved to be a safe heaven and a strategic site between powerful neighboring cities." The Mexica, he argues, made use of this strategic location and established market places and built their city in comparative safety. The second factor according to Townsend was that the Mexica learned the idea of empire from their Tepanec lords during their participation in the conquest of the Tepanec tributary domains. When Mexica were pursuing their own course of action they took advantage of the weakness within the dominant cities and together with the Acolhua and a Tepanec faction took over the empire. The formation of a viable agricultural base with the intensively farmed chinampa system is named as the third factor behind the ascendancy of the Aztec empire (Townsend, 1992 p. 208).

However, Townsend does not adhere to the idea that the management of chinampa zone should be considered the "prime mover" in the rise of the Aztec empire. He posits that the "Aztec states were already well established by the time the great agricultural projects were undertaken" (Townsend, 1992 p. 208).

I find some discrepancies with Townsend's explanation of major factors in Aztec empire building. The chinampas' role and importance in Aztec state formation and empire building did not start with the "great agricultural projects". The projects had certainly a major role in the empire expansion. However, the chinampas were first utilized and expanded by Mexica in that advantageous location, in and around Tenochtitlan. Not withstanding Townsend's discrepancies and his lack of giving credit to chinampas before the "great agricultural projects", Townsend's work is of great value for this chapter of this research project in that he considers the chinampas role in expansion of the Aztec empire as one of the important factors. Townsend's assertion that the chinampas were the third major factor, after the suitability of Tenochtitlan's location and the Mexica's learning the idea of empire from Tepanec suits the contestation of this chapter very well, and I gladly accept his notion of chinampas being the third factor in Aztec empire expansion and use it in this study to further support the importance of the role of chinampas in Aztec empire expansion.

Chinampas as the Main Source of Sustenance for the Aztec Empire

Parsons' (1976) work is very relevant to the research at hand. As we can see from the title of his work, *The Role of Chinampa Agriculture in the Food Supply of Aztec Tenochtitlan*, he is the sole researcher, whom I was able to find, who directly talks about the role of the chinampa agricultural system. Although he concentrated mainly on the chinampas' role in supplying sustenance to the Aztec capital, Tenochtitlan, nevertheless his work is rather unique in his choosing to conduct research specifically on the role of chinampa agriculture. Parsons' work can also be inferred to have a wider implication in the context of the whole Aztec empire, rather than just the capital Tenochtitlan. That is exactly what this research is intending to do.

In his work, Parsons (1976) developed a model of late postclassical food production in the chinampa zone of the Valley of Mexico. A summary of the model is provided in Parsons (1976, pp. 247-248). According to the model, "nucleated" communities were established about 1200 C. E. around the edges of Lake Chalco-Xochimilco. The inhabitants of these settlements constructed chinampas and used local swamp drainage in relatively limited areas, close to the lakeshore and around natural islands. During the Mexica occupancy of the Tenochtitlan some limited drainage and chinampa system were constructed. However, the bulk of the lakebed itself remained as unclaimed swampy area until the later time when the Triple Alliance was formed and Tenochtitlan was well into its development phase. During the late fifteenth century, and the expansion of the Aztec empire and the dominion of Tenochtitlan, large-scale drainage enterprises were planned and constructed within the main Chalco-Xochimilco lakebed. The majority of the older chinampas were also included within the newly constructed large drainage and irrigation system.

The Aztec purpose in undertaking and maintaining these large-scale chinampa cultivation fields was to provide for the subsistence requirements of the inhabitants of Tenochtitlan who were mostly not food producers themselves. The model further suggests that the food supplies from Chalco-Xochimilco chinampas were obtained by Tenochtitlan in three different ways. First, the dependent tenant farmers living in small housing clusters and isolated dwellings that were dispersed throughout the entire chinampa zones of the Tenochtitlan vicinity cultivated roughly 2000 hectares of chinampa land, producing several thousand metric tons of maize, annually. The annual surplus produced by these tenants, which was equivalent of about 2535 metric tons of maize, was appropriated by the officials in Tenochtitlan as "rent". Second, approximately 800 metric tones of grain came to Tenochtitlan in the form of tributes from the non-tenant chinampa growers who dwelled in large, nucleated settlements. Third, these same non-tenant chinampa growers provided Tenochtitlan with about 16, 555 metric tones of maize through the market system (Parsons, 1976, pp. 247-248).

The model further suggests that, during the Aztec empire ascendancy, chinampa cultivation was controlled and managed by the Aztec state through construction and maintenance of large irrigation systems. The construction and management of these systems was principally aimed at providing Tenochtitlan its food needs. With this central policy of the Aztec empire, the chinampa communities of Lake Chalco-Xochimilco gradually grew to be more dependent on Tenochtitlan. This dependency, according to Parson's model, may have been a crucial element in the new level of political authority attained by Tenochtitlan beginning during the fourteenth century and lasting until the Spaniards' arrival (Parsons, 1976, p. 248).

Parsons has clearly shown the necessity of the chinampa agriculture in maintaining Tenochtitlan, the hub of the Aztec empire, and by extension the survival and expansion of the Aztec empire. Parsons' research also weakens the emphasis on the tributary variable role in Tenochtitlan's food supply and the overall supply of Aztec sustenance as suggested by some scholars such as Hicks, (1992) and Barlow (1949). A look at the above figures indicating the amounts of tributary food supplied to Tenochtitlan (800 metric tones), compared to the amounts of food supplied thorough rent and market system (2,535 metric tones through rent and 16,555 metric tones through the market system) clearly shows that the food obtained through tributes composed a very small proportion of the overall food supply of Tenochtitlan.

In his research Harner (1977) discussed the ecological basis for Aztec sacrifice. However, a byproduct of his study is the revelation that the intensification of chinampa agriculture had a unique role to play in sustaining the population pressure in the Valley of Mexico during the Aztec period in light of lack of animal husbandry. According to Harner, "the domesticated animal production was limited by the lack of suitable herbivore... nothing that 'the deer were nearly all killed off' before the Aztec period." (Harner, 1977 pp. 18-119).

From the major works of Armillas (1971), Parsons (1976), and Sanders and others (1979), we clearly know that the Aztecs were involved in the expansion of the chinampa agriculture in the vicinity of Tenochtitlan and the Chalco-Xochimilco area. These chinampa fields were expanded by the Aztecs during the early fifteenth century, the time of the expansion of the Aztec empire, and had a major role in providing sustenance for the populations of Tenochtitlan and surrounding urban centers. The chinampa system also played a major role in the transportation abilities of the Aztecs. Thus we can confidently conclude the important role of chinampa system of agriculture in and around Tenochtitlan, and by inductive reasoning we can generalize the important role of the chinampa agriculture in the whole Aztec empire expansion. Tenochtitlan's status as the main center of the Aztec empire further allows us to use this inductive reasoning in order to establish the important role of the chinampa system of agriculture in Aztec empire building.

Another work that supports the above conclusion is by Sanders (1976). In response to criticism that the irrigation systems based on today's natural spring system were too small and able to supply only fraction of the food supply of Tenochtitlan[11], Sanders (1976 p. 105), provides detailed data on two systems of San Juan Teotihuacan springs and Texcoco Piedmont springs with respect to permanent spring-based irrigation. He concludes that:

> ...The Late Horizon [1350-1521 C.E.] irrigation system could have been at least 1.7 times larger than the recent system, and the Middle Horizon [500-900 C.E.] system approximately twice as large and capable of serving a total of 7,200 hectares of land (Sanders, 1976 pp. 106-107).

---

[11] For the criticism see Wittfogel (1957).

Therefore, Sanders shows that the irrigation systems were capable of supporting a large amount of the food supply of Tenochtitlan.

With respect to man-made canal irrigation, during the Late Horizon [1350-1521 C.E.] Sanders' (1976) survey data "demonstrate the unusual significance of the irrigated land in the Valley in terms of support of large urban communities" (Sanders, 1976 p. 113). This concurs with the findings of Armillas (1971), Sanders and others (1979), and Parsons (1976), in terms of the role and importance of the chinampas in providing the sustenance of Aztec capital, Tenochtitlan.

Calnek (1972), drawing from the works of West and Armillas (1950) and Palerm (1955), characterizes the chinampas as having exceptionally high yields per unit of land. However, he posits that direct substantiation regarding the chinampas actual size, distribution, or economic importance within the valley has been lacking. To remedy this, Calnek embarked on his own study that encompassed the urban settlement pattern and demography, based on colonial period archival sources and "the standard histories and chronicles". The study was initiated at the Archivo General de la Nación (AGN) in Mexico City in 1966. According to Calnek (1972), hundreds of "land titles, land suits, wills and testaments, bills-of-sale" and similar documents pertaining to the occupancy of single residential sites and chinampa gardens in Mexico City (the location of the Aztec capital of Tenochtitlan) have been analyzed. Topographic and demographic information derived from these sources have been used to create a scale map of the city. Contemporary street layouts were revised to approximate the Aztec area situation by discarding streets built since 1521. Aztec era streets that have been shown to exist have been added (Calnek, 1972 p. 105).

The evidence of this project was summarized in Calnek (1972), according to which the evidence implies an exceptionally comprehensive approach to city planning through the major periods of urban growth by the Aztecs of Tenochtitlan. The evidence further indicates that the layout of both individual sites and the entire districts were carefully coordinated with primary as well as secondary streets and canals (Calnek, 1972 p. 111).

Calnek's study indicates that Tenochtitlan was organized through some central authority of the city. The city being the center of the Aztec empire leads us to conclude that it was the Aztec empire central authority that was ultimately responsible for this elaborate city planning. Furthermore, Calnek from his data concluded that no more than a small section of the urban population in Tenochtitlan was engaged in agricultural production. Even large chinampa fields of the southern districts of Tenochtitlan were not sizable enough to support more than a single nuclear family group. From this and other details of his study Calnek concluded that

Tenochtitlan relied on external areas to support its subsistence (Calnek, 1972 p. 114).

Calnek's survey study is in line with Armillas (1971), Sanders and others (1979), and Parsons (1976), in that the Aztec state in order to sustain its urban centers, in this case Tenochtitlan, its largest and most important urban center, had embarked on central planning, using a variety of means including the irrigational constructions to create new chinampa fields and to expand the existing ones in the entire Valley of Mexico. Thus, we can reasonably infer, using inductive reasoning, that the case of Tenochtitlan was also applied to other regions of the Aztec empire and, hence, it is an Aztec phenomenon rather than an isolated case with Tenochtitlan. In any case Tenochtitlan, and by extension the valley of Mexico, was the center of the Aztec empire.

So far our combined sources point to the vital role of chinampas in the sustenance of the Aztec empire as evidently one of the most important variables. Therefore, inferring from these sources, this research endeavor is confident to posit that one of the main variables in Aztec empire building and expansion was that of chinampa agricultural system among other variables such as warfare, religion, markets, and the tributary system, etc. The bulk of scholars, however, point to the latter variables when writing about the Aztec empire.

It is reasonable to assume that the reason behind the lack of a greater number of scholarly works on the specific role and the importance of chinampas in Aztec empire building and expansion is the eminence attached to variables such as warfare, religion, markets, and the tributary system through the sheer volume of scholarly works that have concentrated on these variables rather than the chinampa agriculture in regard to Aztec state formation and empire building and expansion. The possible explanation behind this may be the attractiveness and exotic lure of these variables.

Also chinampa agriculture may have been perceived as a given, so to speak. Scholars may have not thought of investigating about the role of chinampas as much as other variables, thinking that it is self explanatory, and that after acknowledging the initial role of agriculture in sustenance, they should focus on other variables in explaining Aztec empire building and its expansion. But quality researches such as that of Parsons (1976) make it clear that there is a legitimate cause to look at the chinampa system of agriculture and its role in Aztec empire building and expansion.

CHAPTER 6

Conclusion

The subject matter of this research is of immense importance. There are numerous scholarly works on the chinampa agricultural system regarding its history, form, size, productivity and its relevance for today's agricultural sustainability, among many other things. There is no opposition to the fact that the chinampas were used and expanded widely in the Aztec empire period, more than any other period in the history of this system of agriculture. It is then logical to assign an important role to the chinampa agricultural system in most aspects of Aztec life. However, to date the numerous scholarly researches that include chinampa agricultural system, with few exceptions, are limited to the inherent form and qualities of this system. There is a dire need to study the chinampa agricultural system in the context of its role in Aztec empire. Hence, this research has been an important exercise in doing just that, studying the chinampa agricultural system in the context of its role in the Aztec empire.

Following the first chapters of a descriptive nature on the chinampa agricultural system and the history of Aztecs, this research has embarked on finding evidence in support of the hypothesis that the role of the chinampa agriculture was one of the most important elements in the Aztec empire building process. The hypothesis has been holding. This has been accomplished through reviewing several relevant scholarly sources. From these sources inferences have been made in support of the hypothesis in three ways.

The first is through direct evidences provided by the scholars, which literally speak of the important role of the chinampas in Aztec state formation, empire building, and its expansion. Examples of these evidences are provided in chapters 4 and 5 along with the explanation of the importance of those direct evidences in regard to the role of chinampas in Aztec state formation, empire building and expansion.

Second by analysis of the sources this research has made inferences as to the important role of chinampas through inductive reasoning. An important example of this is the inference made from the valuable work of Parson (1976), in which Parson has successfully demonstrated that chinampas were the main source in providing sustenance to Tenochtitlan. The inference by this research is that if chinampas did supply Tenochtitlan, the center of the Aztec empire, then it is reasonable to conclude, in the context of the importance of Tenochtitlan's central position in the Aztec empire (as discussed earlier) that the chinampas were also the means to supply the sustenance of Aztec empire as a whole, and thus they played a major role in sustaining and by extension consolidating and extending the rule of the Aztec empire.

Third, this research has made use of deductive reasoning in inferring the importance of chinampas in Aztec state formation, empire building, and expansion through the analysis of the sources. For example, I have included many sources that confidently have described the major undertaking of the Aztecs in the management of chinampa zones, though construction of large-scale drainage systems among other enterprises. From these managerial efforts of the Aztecs I have made inferences using deductive reasoning that the chinampa agricultural system must have had a crucial role in the Aztecs consolidation of power and its expansion.

Although this research has been successful, in some measure, in establishing the chinampa agricultural system as one of the main factors responsible for the Aztec empire building and expansion, nevertheless, I believe that no single and dominant cause can be found in explaining the processes and causes of the Aztec ascendancy to such great dominion. Rather, the explanation lies in portraying dynamic interactions in the process of social and cultural changes through a variety of causes and variables such as the chinampa agricultural system, religion, warfare, commerce, tribute, etc.

However, in searching for the scholarly sources I have found that variables such as religion, warfare, commerce, and tributary system have taken the bulk of scholars' efforts in explanation of the Aztec empire. I believe it is time that chinampa agricultural system also be studied as rigorously as the other variables. My hope is that this research has shown that the chinampa variable can and should be regarded on a par with other variables so that we can shed a new light in understanding and explaining the Aztec empire building process.

This study should be regarded as a preliminary research study, to test the water so to speak and to look for what is out there in the academic world in terms of works in general on the chinampa system of agriculture as an essential element of the Aztecs' success in empire-building. As such, this study is not complete. It requires much more investigation in terms of both the general history of the empire building of Aztecs as well as the detailed examination of the Aztecs' agricultural systems, particularly the chinampa system, from the very beginning of the Aztec settlements in the swamps until the very end of the empire.

This study has engaged in a preliminary search in uncovering evidence for the hypothesis that the chinampa agricultural system was in fact one of the most essential factors that gradually led the Aztecs to, among other things, pursue their religious ideologies. Driven by those ideologies, they conquered their neighbors and gradually, on one hand, created the Aztec empire, along with all the grand culture, history, artifacts, science, etc. and, on the other hand, caused immense pain and sufferings to their enemies.

REFERENCES

Adams, Robert Mc C. (1960). Early civilizations, subsistence, and environment. In D. Kraeling and R. Adams (eds.) <u>City invincible</u>. Chicago: Oriental institute.

Aguilar, Manuel M. (2006). <u>Handbook to life in the Aztec world</u>. New York: Facts on the file.

Armillas, Pedro (1964). Northern Mesoamerica. In D. J. Jenning and E. Norbeck (eds.), <u>Prehispanic man in the New World</u>. (pp. 291-329), Chicago: University of Chicago Press.

_____ (1971). Gardens on swamps. <u>Science</u>, New Series, Vol. 174 No. 4010 (Nov. 12), 653-661.

Athens, Stephen J. (1977). Theory building and the study of evolutionary process in complex societies. In Binford (ed.), <u>For theory building in archaeology</u> (pp. 353-384), New York: Academic Press.

Avila Lopez, R. (1991). <u>Chinampas de Iztapalapa</u>. D.F. Mexico: Instituto Nacional de Antropologia e Historia.

Barlow, R. H. (1949). The extent of the empire of the Culhua Mexica. Iberamericana, No.28. Berkeley: University of California Press.

Berda, F. Francis (2005). The Aztec of Central Mexico: An imperial society. Belmont, California: Thomson Wadsworth.

Blanton, R. (1972). Prehispanic adaptation in the Ixtapalapa region, Mexico. Science, Vol. 175, 1317-1326.

Boone, Elizabeth H. and T. Commins (1998). Native tradition in the post conquest world. Washington D.C.: Dumbarton Oaks.

Brumfiel, Elizabeth M. (1983). Aztec state making: Ecology, structure, and the origin of the state. American Anthropologist, New Series, Vol. 85, No. 2. (June), 261-284.

Calnek, Edward E. (1972). Settlement pattern and chinampa agriculture at Tenochtitlan. American Antiquity, Vol. 37, No. 1, 104-115.

_____(1974). The Sahagun texts as a source of sociological information. In Munro S. Edmonson (ed.), In sixteenth century Mexico: The work of Sahagun. (pp. 189-204), Albuquerque: University of New Mexico.

Carneiro, Robert L. (1970). A theory of the origin of the state. Science, Vol. 169, 733-738.

Caso, Alfonso (1978). The Aztecs: People of the sun. (Dunhum Lowell, trans.) Norman:

University of Oklahoma (original work published 1958).

Chase-Dunn, Christopher (1991). Review of Ross Hassig's Aztec warfare: Imperial expansion and political control. Comparative Civilization Review Vol. 24 (spring), 101-105.

Coe, M. D. (1964). Chinampas of Mexico. Scientific American Vol. 211, No 1, 90-98.

Conrad, Geoffrey W. and Demarest A. Arthur (1984). Religion and empire: the dynamics of Aztec and Inca expansionism. Cambridge: Cambridge University Press.

Cook, F. S. (1947). The interrelation of population, food supply, and building in pre-conquest Central Mexico. American Antiquity, Vol. 13, No. 1 (July), 45-52.

Cortes, Hernán (1971). Letters from Mexico. A. R. Pagden (trans.), New York: Orion Press

Crossley, Phil (1973). Sub-irrigation in wetland agriculture. Agriculture and Human Value, Vol. 21 191-205.

Davis, Nigel (1973). A history. New York: Putnam's.

Diaz del Castillo, Bernal (1963). The conquest of New Spain. John M. Cohen (trans.), Baltimore: Penguin Books

Duran, Diego (1964). The Aztecs: The history of the Indies of New Spain (1581). Doris Heyden and Fernando Horcasitas. (trans.), New York: Gordon Press.

Engels, Frederick (1972). <u>The Origin of the family, private property, and the state</u>. E. Reed (ed.) Vernon (trans.), New York: Pathfinder Press (original work published 1884).

Evans, Susan T. (1980). Spatial analysis of Basin of Mexico settlement: Problems with the use of the central place model. <u>American Antiquity</u>, Vol. 45, No.4 (Oct.), 866-875.

Fagan, Brian M. (1984). <u>The Aztecs</u>, New York: W. H. Freeman and Company.

Feinman, Gary M. (1997). Presente, passado, y futuro de las chinampas. <u>The Hispanic American Historical Review</u>, Vol. 77, No. 2 (May), 328-329.

Friedman, J. and J. M. Rowland (1978). Notes towards an epigenetic model of the evolution of "civilization". In J. Friedman and J. M. Rowland (eds.), <u>The evolution of social systems</u>. (pp. 201-276), Pittsburg: University of Pittsburg Press.

Gillespie, Susan (1989). <u>The Aztec kings</u>. Tucson: University of Arizona Press.

Hagen, Victor Wolfgang von (1961). <u>The ancient sun kingdoms of the Americas: Aztecs, Maya, Inca</u>. Cleveland and New York: The World Publishing Company.

Harner, Michael (1977). The ecological basis for Aztec sacrifice. <u>American Ethnologist</u>, Vol. 4, No. 1 (Feb.), 117-135

Healan, Dan M. (1989). <u>Tula of the Toltecs</u>. Iowa City: University of Iowa Press.

Hicks, Frederic (1992). Subject state and tribute provinces: The Aztec Empire in the northern Valley of Mexico. Ancient Mesoamerica, Vol. 3, 1-10.

Hole, Frank (1966). Investigating the origin of Mesopotamian Civilization. Science, Vol. 153, 605-611.

Katz, Friedrich (1972). The ancient American civilizations. New York: Praeger.

Keesing, Roger M. (1976). Cultural anthropology: A contemporary perspective. New York: Holt, Reinhart and Winston.

Kirchhoff, Paul (1961). Se puede localizer Aztlan? In Aumario de historia, año. Mexico City: UNAM, Facultad de Fiolsofia y Lettras.

Kottak, Conrad P. (1972). Ecological variables in the origin and evolution of African states: The Buganda example. Comparative Studies in Society and History. Vol. 14, 351-380.

Logan, Michael H. and Sanders, William T. (1976). The natural environment of the Basin of Mexico. In Wolf R. Erik (ed.), The Valley of Mexico: Studies in pre-Hispanic ecology and society. (pp. 31-38), Albuquerque: University of New Mexico.

Michels Joseph W. [Review author] (1973). Prehistoric settlement patterns in the Texcoco Region, Mexico. American Journal of Archaeology, Vol. 77, No.1 (Jan.), 117-118.

Nazareo, Pablo et al. (1941). Carta al Rey don Felipe II...1566. In Francisco del Pasco y Troncoso (ed.), <u>Epistolario de Nueva España</u>. Vol. 10, (pp. 109 - 129), D. F. Mexico: Antigua Liberia Roberdo.

Ojea, F. H. (1897). <u>Libro tercero de la historia religiosa de la provincial de México de la orden de Santo Domingo</u>. Mexico: (n. p.), p. 3.

Outerbridge, Thomas (1987). The disappearing chinampas of Xochimilco. <u>The Ecologist</u>, Vol. 17, 76-83.

Palerm, Angel (1955). The agricultural bases of urban civilization in Mesoamerica. In Jullian Steward (ed.), <u>Irrigation civilizations: A comparative study</u>. Washington: Pan American Union.

_____ (1973). <u>Obras hidraulicas prehispanicas en el sistema lacustre del Valles de Mexico</u>. D. F. Mexico: Instituto Nacional de antropología e Historia.

Parsons, Jeffrey R. (1976). The role of chinampa agriculture in the food supply of Aztec Tenochtitlan. In Cleland E. Charles (ed.), <u>Cultural change and continuity</u>. (pp. 223-257), New York: Academic Press.

Parsons, Jeffrey R., Elizabeth Brumfiel, Mary H. Parsons and David J. Wilson (1982). <u>Prehispanic settlement in the southern Valley of Mexico: The Chalco-Xochimilco region</u>. Michigan: University of Michigan, the Museum of Anthropology.

Parsons, Jeffrey R., M. Parsons, Popper and M. Taft (1985). Chinampa agriculture and Aztec urbanization in the Valley of Mexico. In I.S. Farrington (ed.), Prehistoric intensive agriculture in the tropics. (pp. 49 - 96), Oxford: British Archeological Reports.

Ponce, Padre Alonso (1723). Relación breve y verdadera de algunas cosas de los muchas que sucedieronal Padre Alonso Ponce en las provincias de Nueva España (Madrid), book 13, ch. 32.

Prutzman, Anne C. (1988). The chinampas of the Valley of Mexico. Thesis for Master of Science in Wildlife Resource Science. California: University of California at Berkeley.

Rathje, William L. (1971). The origin and development of lowland classic Maya civilization. American Antiquity, vol. 38, 275-285.

Rojas Rabiela, Teresa (1985). La Tecnologia Agricola Mesoamericana en la siglo XVI. In Teresa Rojas Rabiela, and William T.Sanders (eds.), Historia de la agricultura: Epoca prehispanica siglo XVI, Vol. 1 (pp. 129-231), Mexico City D. F.: Instituto Nacional de antropología e Historia.

_____(ed.).(1993). La agricultura chinampa: complicacion historica. Mexico, D.F.: Universidad Autonoma Chapingo.

_____ (1993). La Tecnologia indigena de construccion de Chinampas en la Cuenca de Mexico. In T. Rojas Rabiela (ed.) La agricultura chinampa: complicacion historica.

(pp. 301-327), Mexico, D.F.: Universidad Autonoma Chapingo.

Sanders, William, T., Jeffrey R. Parsons, and Robert S. Santley (1979). The Basin of Mexico: Ecological process in the evolution of a civilization. New York: Academic Press.

Sanders, William T. and Barbara J. Price (1968). Mesoamerica: The evolution of civilization. New York: Random House.

Sanders William T. (1968). Hydraulic agriculture, economic symbiosis, and the evolution of states in Central Mexico. In B. Meggers (ed.), Anthropological archeology in the Americas. (pp. 88-107), Washington D.C. : Anthropological Society of Washington.

_____(1965). The cultural ecology of the Teotihuacan Valley. Pennsylvania: Pennsylvania State University, Department of Anthropology.

_____(1956). The central Mexican symbiotic region. In G. Willey (ed.) Prehistoric settlement patterns in New World. (pp. 115-127), New York: Werne-Gren Foundation for Anthropological Research. Viking Fund Publications in Anthropology, No 23.

Santley, Robert S. (1980). Disembedded capitals reconsidered. American Antiquity. Vol.45 132-145

Service, Elman R. (1975). Origin of state and civilization. New York: Norton.

Serra Puche, M. C. (1988). Los Recursos lacustra de la Cuenca de Mexico durante el formative Mexico. Mexico D.F. : Universidad Nacional Autonoma de México.

Sluyter, Andrew (1994). Intensive wetland agriculture in Mesoamerica: Space, time, and form. Annals of the Association of American Geographers, Vol. 84. No. 4 (Dec.), 557-584.

Smith, Michael E. (1983). Post classic culture change in Western Morelos. Mexico: The development and correlation of archaeological and Ethnohistorical chronologies. Ph.D. dissertation, Department of Anthropology, University of Illinois.

_____(1986). The role of social stratification in the Aztec Empire: A View from the provinces. American Anthropologist, New Series, Vol. 88, N.1, 70-91.

Smith, Michael E. and Jeffrey T. Price (1994). Aztec-period agricultural terraces in Morales, Mexico: Evidence of household level agricultural intensification. Journal of Field Archaeology, Vol. 21, No.2 (summer), 169 - 179.

Smith, Robert H. (ed.) (1992). Aztecs: Reign of blood and splendor. Alexandria, Virginia: Time-Life Books.

Steward, Julian H. (1949). Cultural causality and law: A trial formulation of the development of early civilizations. American Anthropologist, Vol. 51, 1-27.

Toquemada, Fr. J. de (1723). <u>Monarquia Indiana</u> (Madrid) Book 13 ch., 32.

Townsend, F. Richard (1992). <u>The Aztecs</u>. New York: Thames and Hudson.

Vargas Machuca, B. de. (1599). <u>Melicia y descripción de las Yndias,</u> (Madrid).

Werner, Louis (1992). Cultivating the secret of Aztec gardens. <u>Americas,</u> vol. 44 Issue 6 (Nov. /Dec), 6-16.

West, R. C. and P. Armillas (1950). Las chinampas de Mexico. <u>Cuadernos Americanos,</u> Vol. 50, 165-182.

Wilken, Gene (1985). "A note on buoyancy and other dubious characteristics of the 'floating' chinampas of Mexico. In I. S. Farrington (ed.), <u>Prehistoric intensive agriculture in the tropics.</u> (pp. 31-48), Oxford: British Archeological Reports, Vol. 232, i and ii.

Wittfogel, Karl A. (1957). <u>Oriental despotism: A comparative study of total power</u>. New Haven: Yale University Press.

Wright, Henry T. (1978). Toward an explanation o the origins of the state. In R. Cohen and E. Service (eds.). <u>Origins of the state: The anthropology of political evolution.</u> (pp. 49-68), Philadelphia: Institute for the Study of Human Issues.

Yoffee, Norman (1979). The decline and rise of Mesopotamian civilization: An ethnoarchaeological perspective on the evolution of social complexity. <u>American Antiquity</u>, Vol. 44, 5-35.

9562506R00072

Printed in Great Britain
by Amazon.co.uk, Ltd.,
Marston Gate.